Democratic Socialism
on
Trial

This book is a work of political analysis. No part of this book may be reproduced, stored in a retrieval system, or transmitted in any form or by any means, including electronic, mechanical, photocopying, microfilming, recording, or otherwise (except for that copying permitted by sections 107 and 108 of the United States Copyright Law and expect by reviewers for the public press), without written permission from the Publisher.

Germinal G. Van

DEMOCRATIC SOCIALISM ON TRIAL

Why It Won't Work In America

Kindle Direct Publishing

Table of Contents

Books Published by the same Author

American Political Culture: An Observation From The Outside

Equal Under The Law: A Reflection on Amendment XIV and the Concept of Citizenship

Essay On Issues: The Fundamentals of American Politics (Volume 1)

Reflection On Identity Politics: Here Is Why It Divides More Than It Unites

The Efficiency of Capitalism: The Economic and Political Philosophy of the Free-Market

Preface

Most of my friends are left-wing. The majority of them are socialists. It is great that they hold views that are diametrically opposed to mine. It is fascinating to see how they still adamantly believe that socialism can still work although evidence show its failure all around the world. My friends are not alone in their delusive belief on socialism. Many people do still believe in socialism because they resent capitalism. They hold that capitalism is the foundation of the woes of society. People are suffering because of capitalism although the contrary has been proven...people do suffer more under socialism. Lenin, Stalin, Mao, Pol Pot, Mugabé, and Nicolae Ceaucescu are examples of political leaders who have butchered their own people in the name of socialism. Moreover, socialism had brought more people into poverty.

In America, asserting that one is socialist is generally not well perceive by the court of public opinion. So democratic socialism has become the new trend to spread the ideas of socialism around. Those who defend democratic socialism argue that it is substantively different than socialism, because democracy plays a huge role in the process. As a matter of fact, democratic socialism is not different than socialism, because democracy is not, in the first place, compatible with socialism. Democratic socialism is simply a pretext to advance socialism in the United States. Nonetheless, democratic socialism will never work in America because its purpose is to eradicate capitalism, private property and human flourishing. This book was written with the motivation to demonstrate to those who advocate for democratic socialism that, that ideology is a false and unfeasible ideology as socialism itself is.

Whether it is democratic socialism, socialism, or communism, a political system that seeks to collectivize resources is doomed to fail regardless of how it is implemented because the confiscation of knowledge and private property intrinsically preclude human progress. Collectivizing resources benefits no one but only those who decide how resources should be collectivized, which means those who rule the state. Human beings are naturally inclined to keep the profit of what they have produced. So, confiscating the benefits of someone's production, and put that benefits up for public use is the first step toward the failure and decline of collectivization. That is why collectivization never works, and the American people clearly understood that. Democratic socialism is doomed to fail, and it will never work whether it is in America or anywhere else.

Introduction

I rather be honest from the get-go with the reader than pretending something else. I see democratic socialism as the greatest falsehood in political theory and political philosophy. It is the greatest demagoguery spread in politics during election time. It is a mask that attempts to revive socialism—an ideology that has previously failed and will continue to fail because it is an adversarial ideology to human nature. The most famous quote "All men were born equal" pronounced in the American Declaration of Independence and in the Declaration of the Rights of Man and the Citizen, has been misinterpreted in all shapes and forms by the proponents of egalitarian politics. Egalitarian politics has been growing in the United States under the guise of democratic socialism, within the aim of achieving ultimate equality among human beings.

However, the expansion of this false ideology is gaining support and influence within the youth in the universities and even in high schools. Many individuals have begun to espouse the premises of this ideology as the main alternative to combat capitalism in the United States, without thoroughly understand the substance it contains. The United States is, first and foremost, a liberal democracy within a constitutional republic. A liberal democracy because the rights of the individual are preserved and promulgated; and a republic because the institutions that encompass the government are free and independent from one another. The strength of the American republic lies in the limited amount of power it gave to its government, which entails that its people are freer. In a state build upon socialist values, the people are not free. They are enslaved by the bureaucracy and the predatory power of government.

I do see democratic socialism as a threat to individual rights and liberties in America. I perceive it as the trigger of a societal decay, and the detonator of a prospective dictatorship of left-wing politics. That is why I was determined to write this book. I deemed necessary to warn society through my writings regarding the menace of this dangerous ideology on the rise. Democratic socialism may sound good and fair on paper because it advocates for social justice, fairness, and equality against the unjust outcomes of capitalism; nonetheless, its implementation would be characteristically destructive and apocalyptic for a free society like the United States. This book was also written to make the reader understand that a political ideology that advocates for a central authority to control the means of production, is an ideology that aims to enslave mankind, to deprive individuals of their liberties and property; and to ensconce societal decay.

The book is divided into two major parts. The first part essentially concentrates on the nature of democratic socialism as a political doctrine and the second part articulates on the reasons of the inapplicability of democratic socialism in the United States. To explicitly elaborate upon the nature of democratic socialism, the first part of the book has been split into four chapters. The first chapter entitled "What is Democratic Socialism?" provides an overview of democratic socialism as a political doctrine. The second chapter entitled "The Arbitrary Nature of Democratic Socialism" explains in depth, the coercive essence of democratic socialism in the modern state. The third chapter entitled "The Failure of Socialism as a Warning," attempts to warn the reader about the deceptive nature of democratic socialism through the failure of socialism as a political regime in countries and regions like the Soviet Union, Eastern Europe, Vietnam, or Cuba. The fourth chapter entitled "Communism: The Logical Fallacy of Karl Marx," gives an account of communism as a political doctrine fundamentally antagonistic to human nature. It explicates how Karl Marx has misjudged human nature by thinking that collectivism would be the answer to attenuate inequality.

The second part of the book is divided into four main chapters. The first chapter of the second part, which is named "The Roots of Libertarianism and Egalitarianism In America" epitomizes the points that spotlight the essence of the two ideologies as intrinsic political philosophies in

American political culture. It extends the rationale behind the rise of democratic socialism in the United States as an alternative to capitalism. The fifth chapter titled "Bernie Sanders: A Threat to Liberty and a Danger to Our Republic" argues the dangerous policies of United States Senator Bernie Sanders such as the proposals for a single-payer healthcare system, free-education or job-guaranteed to everyone; and the harmful consequences it could potentially have on American society. The sixth and last chapter of the book is entitled "The Dictatorship of The Minority: The Subversion of Liberty for An Egalitarian Society." It emphasizes on the how minority groups are dictating and controlling society through the notions of identity politics and political correctness, and how democratic socialism has become progressively the regime of hope and equality in which proponents of liberalism, progressivism and globalism want to create. The last chapter is the conclusion of the book. It summarizes the whole argument of the premise as of why democratic socialism is doomed to fail.

PART ONE

THE NATURE OF DEMOCRATIC SOCIALISM

ONE

What Democratic Socialism Is?

Democratic socialism is a political philosophy that advocates for political democracy alongside social ownership of the means of production with an emphasis on self-management and democratic management of economic institutions.[1] Democratic socialists hold that capitalism is inherently incompatible with what they hold to be the democratic values of liberty, equality and solidarity.[2] The main feature about democratic socialism is that it sounds good, and fair on paper, like the way socialism and communism respectively sound and appeal. But the hard truth is that it does not work because it is incompatible with the human condition as a way to control the means of production. Each of

---

[1] Busky, Donald F. *Democratic Socialism: A Global Survey.* (2000). Praeger. Pp.7-8. ISBN: 978-0275968861. "Democratic socialist is the wing of the socialist movement that combines a belief in a socially owned economy with that of political democracy.
[2] Busky, Ibid.

these political doctrines appeal on egalitarian philosophy by which the government is the central and supreme entity that regulates the life of the individual as well as equality. It is very quintessential to comprehend that the demand for equality equates the diminution and subsequent suppression of freedom. Famous Russian writer and essayist, Aleksandr Solzhenitsyn once asseverated that "Human beings are born with different capacities. If they are free, they are not equal. And if they are equal, they are not free."[3] Democratic socialism does not seek to guarantee nor to preserve the liberty of individuals but to strictly control individuals coercively by expanding egalitarian politics and policies. Expanding egalitarian politics and policies entails an amplification of unfair redistributive policies.

---

[3] Aleksandr Solzhenitsyn quote on liberty.

To understand the core nature of democratic socialism, one must comprehend how welfare is or will be used under such regime. Under a democratic socialist regime, the government will attempt to subsidize private entrepreneurship by enlarging the welfare state. Democratic socialists believe that there are some reforms that empower and embolden the working-class to fight battles in other areas.[4] To the democratic socialists, governmental social programs ameliorate the human condition of the collectivity as a whole instead of using a laissez-faire economic system which favors competition and inequality. In the United States, when democratic socialists argue about the plausibility, feasibility and applicability of the issues that they are advocating for (Medicare-

---

[4] Day, Meagan, "Democratic Socialism, Explained by a Democratic socialist" *Vox.* August 1, 2018, *https://www.vox.com/first-person/2018/8/1/17637028/bernie-sanders-alexandria-ocasio-cortez-cynthia-nixon-democratic-socialism-jacobin-dsa*. Article. Web.

For-All, free-tuition for college students, free housing…etc.); they use Canada, and principally Scandinavia (Norway, Sweden, Finland, Denmark and Iceland) as examples and justification for their premise. They [democratic socialists] confuse the social democracy's precepts for democratic socialist ideals. Canada, and Scandinavian nations have a social democratic form of political regime and not a democratic socialist political regime as they may want to portray it. Social democracy emphasizes on having a capitalistic economy with a gigantic social welfare system. The reason why these countries are enabled to enforce redistributive policies is because they are constitutional representative democracies; they have extensive welfare benefits, corporatist collective bargaining between labor and capital that is managed by the state, and some state ownership of the economy.[5] In social democracies, public ownership of the main productive assets is limited in comparison to what it could be.[6] As a matter of fact, if we take the case of Norway; the Norwegian government owns seventy-four companies.[7] It signifies that they are about 2.8 million total employed workers in Norway—just 10 percent of the employed workforce in these state-owned enterprises.[8] Within social democracies, which are the most government-intervention economies in capitalistic systems, the public sector employs about 30 percent of the workforce, which is the highest proportion in the capitalist world.[9]

---

[5] McCarthy, Michael A., "Democratic Socialism Isn't Social Democracy", *Jacobin*, August, 7, 2018. *https://jacobinmag.com/2018/08/democratic-socialism-social-democracy-nordic-countries*. Article. Web.
[6] McCarthy, Ibid.
[7] McCarthy, Ibid.
[8] McCarthy, Ibid.
[9] McCarthy, Ibid.

Unlike social democracy, which relies upon a capitalistic economy to ensconce public ownership, democratic socialism is anti-capitalistic. Its economic philosophy rests on the fact that resources and labor are distributed according to what society, whether that be through means like state or planning committees, deems appropriate.[10] The main problem with democratic socialism is that it points out social problems, promises an utopian outcome without offering concrete solution on how to achieve those goals. Indeed, it proposed simple solutions to complex problems like the way nationalism does. The actual general philosophy of democratic socialism is based in an anti-capitalist planned economy.[11] That is not how the Nordic model

---

[10] Stadelman, Austin, "Don't confuse Social Democracy and Democratic Socialism", *The Daily Illini*, September 5, 2018. https://dailyillini.com/opinions/2018/09/05/dont-confuse-social-democracy-and-democratic-socialism/, Article. Web.
[11] Stadelman, Ibid.

operates, because it supports free trade and the movement of goods based on liberal economic theory.[12] Those who identify themselves as democratic socialist like Alexandria Ocasio-Cortez, or Bernie Sanders; are, in fact, advocates for social democracy without being aware that they actually are. The worst is that, they think that they are championing democratic socialism principles, but they do it without thoroughly comprehending the substance of the ideology they are defending. If they are truly aware and cognizant of the fact that they are advocating for socialism, they are, then, purposefully fooling the masses for the sake of holding power.

---

[12] Stadelman, Ibid.

References

Busky, Donald F. *Democratic Socialism: A Global Survey.* (2000). Praeger. Pp.7-8. ISBN: 978-0275968861. "Democratic socialist is the wing of the socialist movement that combines a belief in a socially owned economy with that of political democracy.

Busky, Ibid.

Aleksandr Solzhenitsyn quote on liberty.

Day, Meagan, "Democratic Socialism, Explained by a Democratic socialist" Vox. August 1, 2018, https://www.vox.com/first-person/2018/8/1/17637028/bernie-sanders-alexandria-ocasio-cortez-cynthia-nixon-democratic-socialism-jacobin-dsa. Article. Web.

McCarthy, Michael A., "Democratic Socialism Isn't Social Democracy", Jacobin, August, 7, 2018. https://jacobinmag.com/2018/08/democratic-socialism-social-democracy-nordic-countries. Article. Web.

McCarthy, Ibid.

McCarthy, Ibid.

McCarthy, Ibid.

McCarthy, Ibid.

Stadelman, Austin, "Don't confuse Social Democracy and Democratic Socialism", The Daily Illini, September 5, 2018. https://dailyillini.com/opinions/2018/09/05/dont-confuse-social-democracy-and-democratic-socialism/, Article. Web.

Stadelman, Ibid.

Stadelman, Ibid.

TWO

The Arbitrary Nature of Democratic Socialism

We live in dangerous times. We live in times where this fallacious ideology [democratic socialism] is growing and expanding within the American youth. Many college students supported Bernie Sanders during the 2016 presidential elections, and many more supported Alexandria Ocasio-Cortez when she ran for Congress in 2018 on a democratic socialist platform. It is very interesting to see that within the American population; democratic socialism appeals to millennials than those who are surely over age thirty or thirty-five. We thought that socialism as a political ideology was dead because of the ultimate dissolution of the Soviet Union in 1991. Apparently, it has been rehabilitated into classrooms by liberal and progressive professors who attempt to indoctrinate college students to espouse radical left-wing policies. Of course, champions of democratic socialism have targeted college campuses because millennials are easy to be politically manipulated. Of course, most college students and the American youth in general, are flattered when they hear "free college-tuition for every student in the United States," and "Medicare for all" — and the champions of democratic socialism acutely narrow that narrative to sustain their ideological basis among those college students. Notwithstanding the fact that democratic socialism sounds good in theory, its proponents do not enunciate its arbitrary and unjust nature. The American youth overall, and college students in particular, have been deprived of the truth regarding democratic socialism. Democratic socialism has an arbitrary, darker, vicious, and I would even go further by saying; a brutal nature than the one it may want to portray.

The arbitrary nature of democratic socialism is logically authoritarian and oppressive. The roots of the oppressiveness of the socialist state are entrenched in paranoia. This paranoia is about imaginary saboteurs, wreckers, hoarders, traitors and speculators. These phantoms are always accused of undermining the economy.[13] More generally, the oppressive character of socialist societies was generally linked to the economic requirements of a centrally-planned economy.[14] The anti-capitalistic approach of democratic socialism is primarily to over-expand the power of government, which inevitably leads to the deprivation, and the suppression of individual liberties. In a free-market

-----

[13] Niemietz, Kristian, "Introduction: Socialism is Popular—but only in the abstract", The Mirage of Democratic Socialism, IEA Discussion Paper No92. August 2018. https://iea.org.uk/wp-content/uploads/2018/08/The-Mirage-of-Democratic-Socialism-An-Alternative-History_web.pdf. Opinion.
[14] Niemietz, Ibid.

society, the individual is king, and the government is his servant. A society based upon a free-market and laissez-faire economy gives more autonomy to the individuals to contribute to society's advancement. It promulgates competition which subsequently stimulates wealth. A free-market society like the one we have in the United States, requires a strongly constrained, restricted and limited government intervention into the economy. The wealth of a society is grounded upon how much involvement does the government have over the economy. Furthermore, the fundamental element of free-market is liberty because if individuals are not free to pursue their self-interests, they cannot create, innovate, nor expand resources; which are critical features for the advancement of the human condition. Milton Friedman, an American economist, a Nobel Prize-winner and a prominent advocate of laissez-faire economics, once said: *"A society that puts equality before freedom will get neither. A society that puts freedom before equality will get a high degree of both."*[15] That quote alone sums up the route that a society should undertake in order to achieve economic prosperity. However, democratic socialism supports the utter opposite of laissez-faire economics. It advocates for a world where capitalism would be abolished, and where the means of production would be socially owned. Something that is owned by everyone therefore belongs to no one. If it belongs to no one, thus, it has no value; because value is grounded in ownership, and democratic socialism rejects ownership.

In a democratic socialist society, equality is enhanced before liberty. The problem with enhancing equality over liberty is that—prioritizing

---

[15] Milton Friedman Quote.

equality over liberty requires the government to be more involved in people's live, which therefore means; a more interventionist and intrusive governmental attitude. This accentuation of government-intervention into the economy empowers the government to determine prices as well as the means of production, and under what conditions the economy should be stimulated. The economic system of a democratic socialist government is rooted into an unfair redistribution of resources under the pretext of social justice, which indicates that it uses the money of the wealthy individuals to give it to the poor people because it is morally the right thing to do. However, it is not because something is morally right that it is necessarily legally, empirically and factually valid. While unjustly taking that money from the wealthy man who earned his money through hard-work, in order to give it to the "disadvantaged," the democratic socialist government does not do any favor to the disadvantaged person. Instead, it creates a system of tangible public assistance, dependency and entitlement. Under a democratic socialist government, the human condition is attached and dependent on welfare benefits. This dependency onto welfare generates societal laziness, and a strong denial of personal responsibility. Incrementally, it exponentially increases the authority of the government in deciding for man instead of man deciding for himself.

If freedom means the absence of coercion, then those are freer who are less coerced.[16] Equality, on the other hand, means necessary the use of coercion from the government to ensure an equal

---

[16] Bovard, James, "Liberty vs. Equality" Foundation for Economic Education, October 1, 1977. https://fee.org/articles/liberty-vs-equality/. Article. Web.

result. Equality before the law does not require coercion because individuals are all held accountable to their actions before the rule of law. But equality of economic outcome does require coercion. Under a democratic socialist system, equality is in clear conflict with liberty.[17] Indeed, it aims at enforcing equality of outcome. This concept of equality differs from equality under the law and equality of opportunities. Government measures to achieve fair shares for all, reduce liberty—if what people get is determined by fairness, then who is to decide what is fair?[18] If what people get is determined by fairness and not by what they produce, where are the prizes to come from? What

---

[17] Port Douglas, "Milton Friedman Essay on Equality and Liberty". May 31, 2018, https://douglasportmba.com/2018/05/31/milton-friedman-essay-on-equality-and-liberty/. Essay. Web.
[18] Boyard, Ibid.

incentive is there to work and produce?[19] If it is the government to decide what is fair, then it [the government] becomes an arbitrary and coercive power that relies upon an authoritative approach to achieve production. The fundamental conflict between the ideal of fair shares and the ideal of personal liberty has plagued every attempt to make equality of outcome the overriding principle of social organization.[20]

The aim to achieve equality of outcome under a democratic socialist regime is inherently fallacious. Let's say a socialist government has to choose between only two ends: greater income equality or greater racial justice—it has to define clearly what equality and justice mean in terms that everyone can

---

[19] Boyard, Ibid.
[20] Boyard, Ibid.

agree on.[21] What counts as income? What constitutes racial justice?[22] At what point has equality been achieved or justice served: perfect equality or perfect justice?[23] Under such circumstances, the fewer the people who have input into the final plan, the better—that's why if the idea of democracy embodies the liberal ideals of self-direction, of enabling ordinary people to meaningfully choose the policies that will rule them, and of self-expression, then democracy poses an insurmountable problem for socialism.[24] That is why democratic socialism etymologically speaking, is an oxymoron, and ideologically contradictory. More socialism simply means less democracy because the

---

[21] Ikeda, Sandy, "Democratic Socialism Is a Contradiction in Terms", Foundation for Economic Education, March 17, 2016, https://fee.org/articles/democratic-socialism-is-a-contradiction-in-terms/. Article. Web.
[22] Ikeda, Ibid.
[23] Ikeda, Ibid.
[24] Ikeda, Ibid.

more coercive control government exercises, the less self-direction there can be.[25] Under a democratic socialist regime, government planning manages personal planning, the sphere of personal autonomy weakens and shrinks, and the sphere of governmental authority strengthens and expands.[26] Incrementally, democratic socialism is not a doctrine designed to protect the liberal values of democracy—it is a doctrine created to force those of us who cherish those liberal values onto a slippery slope toward tyranny.[27]

---

[25] Ikeda, Ibid.
[26] Ikeda, Ibid.
[27] Ikeda, Ibid.

References

Niemietz, Kristian, "Introduction: Socialism is Popular—but only in the abstract", The Mirage of Democratic Socialism, IEA Discussion Paper No92. August 2018. https://iea.org.uk/wp-content/uploads/2018/08/The-Mirage-of-Democratic-Socialism-An-Alternative-History_web.pdf. Opinion.

Niemietz, Ibid.

Milton Friedman Quote.

Bovard, James, "Liberty vs. Equality" Foundation for Economic Education, October 1, 1977. https://fee.org/articles/liberty-vs-equality/. Article. Web.

Port Douglas, "Milton Friedman Essay on Equality and Liberty". May 31, 2018, https://douglasportmba.com/2018/05/31/milton-friedman-essay-on-equality-and-liberty/. Essay. Web.

Boyard, Ibid.

Boyard, Ibid.

Boyard, Ibid.

Ikeda, Sandy, "Democratic Socialism Is a Contradiction in Terms", Foundation for Economic Education, March 17, 2016, https://fee.org/articles/democratic-socialism-is-a-contradiction-in-terms/. Article. Web.

Ikeda, Ibid.

Ikeda, Ibid.

Ikeda, Ibid.

Ikeda, Ibid.

Ikeda, Ibid.

Ikeda, Ibid.

THREE

The Failure of
Socialism
As a Warning

Every nation-state that has attempted to use of socialism or communism as a political regime and as an economic system—has declared bankruptcy or has deliberately failed as an economic power. It was the case for the Soviet Union, Southeast Asia, Cuba, Venezuela, Mozambique, Angola, Tanzania, Chile in the early 1970s, and the communist Eastern European satellite states of the Soviet Union. All these geopolitical states have failed to deliver on the promises of socialism and communism. Their failure has substantiated the fact that socialism is truly the product society's utopia. And a utopia by mere definition is an imaginary place wherein everything is perfect and immaculate. If socialism, which is the intermediary step to attain communism, has failed to prevail as a political regime and as an economic doctrine, then what is the substantial difference which guarantees the sustainability and the prevalence of democratic socialism in relation to that of socialism? The answer is: none! There is no substantial difference between the two because one is the other—therefore, it will deliver the same result, which is the failure to sustain and to prevail. I am going to use three countries to demonstrate how socialism has failed in the past and how it will still fail if it was rehabilitated under the label of "Democratic Socialism."

The first country to exemplify the failure of socialism is no other than the Soviet Union. Indeed, the Soviet Union was the very first country in geopolitics to incorporate socialism as a political regime and as an economic model. Before the creation of the Soviet Union, socialism was only an ideal, a theoretical framework conscientiously and meticulously written by Karl Marx and Friedrich

Engels in the 1848-book, entitled *The Communist Manifesto*. I personally believe that *The Communist Manifesto* was probably the most powerful book ever written by men after the Bible and the Quran. This pamphlet professed the ultimate egalitarian and classless society in which capitalism would be utterly destroyed, private property would be abolished, and the proletariat would govern the bourgeoisie with an iron fist. Moreover, the communist ideal asserted that the economic prosperity of a classless society can only be achieved through a government central-planning economy before it withers away as Marx predicted. The Bolsheviks and their political leader, Vladimir Illich Ulyanov better known as Lenin—led a bloody revolution wherein the people (the proletariat) would overthrow the aristocratic regime of the tsar, a regime that has ruled Russia for centuries based on social inequality. The purpose of the Russian Revolution was to create a new society—a classless society like it was envisioned in *The Communist Manifesto*. In creating the new Russian state which would become Soviet Russia then the Soviet Union under Stalin, Lenin was determined to become the first political leader to apply Marxist doctrines into practice. However, the new Bolshevik government became rapidly authoritarian and exponentially totalitarian. Private property was obliterated, public ownership and the means of production were entirely controlled by the Soviet government. Furthermore, the independence of the judiciary was also under government control, which indicates that the Russian (Bolshevik) judiciary simply became an instrument of the political police of the Bolshevik Russian State. Within the Bolshevik Russian State, due process of law was nearly non-existent—any individual suspected of being an enemy of the Bolshevik State was prosecuted and subsequently executed by the political police of Lenin. The political climate worsened in Soviet Russia when Lenin died, and Stalin seized power. Stalin was the most powerful dictator of the twentieth century and was the most powerful leader of the largest communist state on earth. Nonetheless, he was the most murderous political leader of the century. Under Stalin rule, the Bolshevik Russian State has expanded in becoming the Soviet Union. For the bourgeois classes everywhere, the inauguration of the Soviet regime was anathema to core values of the western civilization, while for radicals and communists; it signified a natural culmination of the inevitable march of history toward human freedom and social order devoid of exploitation.[28] The end of World War II promulgated the Soviet Union to become a superpower whose industrial strength was equal to that of the United States at some point in history. Despite having dominated half of Europe for half a century, socialism and communism have fallen. They have failed as an economic doctrine, and as a political regime. Originally, the socialist ideal was that state ownership and scientific planning would replace the anarchy of the market.[29] Material benefits would accrue to the working-class; an equitable economy would supplant capitalist exploitation and a new socialist man would rise,

---

[28] Polychroniou, C J, "The Failed Dream of a Russian Revolution" Aljazeera, October 25, 2017, https://www.aljazeera.com/indepth/opinion/failed-dream-russian-revolution-171018082225358.html. Article. Web.
[29] Gregory, Paul R. "Why Socialism Fails", Defining Ideas, Hoover Institution Journal, The Hoover Institution, January 10, 2018, https://www.hoover.org/research/why-socialism-fails. Article. Web.

prioritizing social above private interests; a dictatorship of the proletariat would guarantee the interests of the working-class.[30] The economic failure of the Soviet Union was primarily based upon the fact that the Soviet state competed in a nuclear arm race with the United States throughout the twentieth century, without having the adequate resources to sustain its economy. It produced more nuclear weapons than the economic resources could supply. Unable to fulfill the economic demands to obtain a product of quality, Soviet nuclear missiles were considerably outnumbered and outmoded to those of the United States. Secondly, the economic failure of the Soviet Union was rooted in its system of material-balance planning. Indeed, material-balance planning was the fundamental weakness of the

---

[30] Gregory, Ibid.

Soviet system.[31] Material-balance planning is, first and foremost, a method of economic planning where material supplies are accounted for in natural units and use to balance the supply of available inputs with targeted outputs.[32] This system defaulted the Soviet economic system because the Soviet system was based on output plans. One enterprise's output was another's input.[33] If output plans failed widely, the whole plan would fail.[34] Material-balance planning was hostile to new products and new technologies because they required a reworking of an already fragile system of balances.[35] Communism

---

[31] Gregory, Ibid.

[32] Gregory and Stuart, Comparing Economic System in the Twenty-First Century, 2003. ISBN 0-618-26181-8. P.127.

[33] Gregory, Paul R. "Why Socialism Fails", Defining Ideas, Hoover Institution Journal, The Hoover Institution, January 10, 2018, https://www.hoover.org/research/why-socialism-fails. Article. Web.

[34] Gregory, Ibid.

[35] Gregory, Ibid.

has also failed as a political regime in the Soviet Union. The greatest factor that triggered the decline of Soviet socialism is none other than a person with the name of Gorbachev. Mikhail Sergeyevich Gorbachev was the last Soviet Premier. He [Gorbachev] came to power with a set of economic and political reforms which the Soviets were not habituated to. These reforms can be summarized as the *Perestroika* which means liberalization of the Soviet economic system, and *Glasnost*, which is the openness and transparency of the Soviet government. I am going to focus on the "Glasnost" policy of Gorbachev because it was the principal policy of government reforms. Before Glasnost was effectively invigorated; Eastern Europe, which was under Soviet domination, practiced a policy of closure in which the policies administered in these Eastern European countries, were directly decided from the Kremlin. The effectuation of Glasnost has had a domestic and foreign impact on the collapse of the Soviet Union. The domestic impact was that it has authorized the freedom of press, as well as the creation of political pluralism. On the foreign aspect, the Glasnost policy has allowed Eastern European countries to create their own society as they see fit without Soviet interference. In other words, the Glasnost policy has promulgated the right to self-determination in Eastern Europe. The truth is that, Gorbachev did not administer the Glasnost policy because he wanted to give Eastern Europe its freedom. He did so because the empire was too expensive to maintain.[36] Consequently, restraints were loosened and the communist leaders in Eastern

---

[36] Palmer, Tom G. "Why Socialism Collapsed in Eastern Europe", Cato Institute, October 1990, https://www.cato.org/publications/commentary/why-socialism-collapsed-eastern-europe. Article, Web.

Europe were told that they would get no further support from the Kremlin.[37] Mere power is usually not enough to sustain a tyrannical regime—in the Soviet Union, the rulers claimed to act on behalf of the proletariat.[38] Soviet rulers thought that they were morally justified, that they were acting in the interests of the working-class, but all they truly wanted was power and privilege at the expense of the working-class.[39] The socialist ideology in the Soviet Union promised equality, fraternity, and prosperity, but utterly failed to deliver on those promises. For instance, if we compare the standard of living of the average citizen of East Germany, the richest of the fraternal nations of the socialist camp, with that of the party members who lived in Wandlitz, the neighborhood of the party elite, we

---

[37] Palmer, Ibid.
[38] Palmer, Ibid.
[39] Palmer, Ibid.

find incredible disparities of income—but until recently they were kept secret.[40] These disparities show the hypocrisy of the socialist ideal and its limpid failure.

The second country to epitomize the failure of socialism is Cuba. The eminent Cuban socialist leader, Fidel Castro also wanted to apply Marxist principles of socialism based on the Soviet model. After the overthrow of Fulgencio Batista, who was an ally of the United States government, Fidel Castro, a convinced Marxist-Leninist socialist, became the strongman of the Cuban state. Castro was a staunch believer in the Marxist prophecy of socialism. He firmly believed that a more just society was feasible and practicable under the doctrines of socialism. To achieve that goal, like the Soviet Union, Castro made of Cuba a one-party communist state,

---

[40] Palmer, Ibid.

while industries and businesses were nationalized and state socialist reforms were implemented throughout the Cuban society.[41] Within its new constitution, it was explicitly stated that "We believe in a socialist, sovereign, independent, prosperous and sustainable country."[42] This constitutional clause was intended to strengthen political institutions and to create a more collective leadership structure.[43] Cuba is replacing its Soviet-era constitution with a new constitution to reflect and implement political and economic changes designed to make its one-party socialist system—

---

[41] Wikipedia Contributors, "Fidel Castro", Wikipedia, the Free Encyclopedia, November 2018, web.

[42] Marsh, Sarah, "Cuba Aims to Build Socialism, Not Communism, In Draft Constitution", Reuters, July 21, 2018, https://www.reuters.com/article/us-cuba-assembly/cuba-aims-to-build-socialism-not-communism-in-draft-constitution-idUSKBN1KB0ML. Article. Web.

[43] Wikipedia Contributors, Ibid.

one of the last in the world- sustainable.[44] The draft of Cuba's new constitution keeps the Communist Party as its leading political force but states as its aim is the construction of socialism rather than communism, reflecting changing times, and top officials.[45] Nevertheless, this attempt at refreshing and renewing Cuba's political system does not erase the previous economic and political failures it has encountered under Castro's socialism. Undoubtedly, socialism in Cuba was a failed experiment. The Cuban socialist revolution was heavily supported by the Soviet Union which was its main economic benefactor. When he took power in 1959, Fidel Castro chose, or was pushed into conflict

---

[44] Editors, "Cuba Aims For Socialism, Not Communism", The Sydney Morning Herald, July 22, 2018, https://www.smh.com.au/world/central-america/cuba-aims-for-socialism-not-communism-20180722-p4zsw5.html. Article. Web.
[45] Editors, Ibid.

with its largest export, the United States.[46] The distant Soviet Union could buy Cuba's principal export; sugar; at guaranteed prices.[47] It could give other forms of economic and technical aid—but it also helped seduce the fledgling revolutionary leaders into imposing a command economy rather than market-driven one.[48] Defending Fidel Castro's economic management became even harder after the collapse of the Soviet empire in the late 1980s.[49] Subsidies stopped, Russia no longer took the sugar crop at guaranteed prices, and the GDP fell by one-third in the early 1990s.[50] The severe economic

---

[46] McRae, Hamish, "Fidel Castro's Cuba Failed Economically-But He Had Little Choice In The Matter", Independent, November 26, 2017, https://www.independent.co.uk/voices/fidel-castro-economy-death-cuba-economics-communism-a7441066.html. Article. Web.
[47] McRae, Ibid.
[48] McRae, Ibid.
[49] McRae, Ibid.
[50] McRae, Ibid.

stagnation forced many Cuban citizens to flee Cuba for the United States, in order to avoid famine. As historian Archie Brown would say about socialism, he noted: "The idea of building communism, a society in which the state would have withered away, turned out to be a dangerous illusion. What was built instead was Communism, an oppressive party-state which was authoritarian at best and ruthlessly totalitarian at worst."[51] Besides political centralization, the failed ideas of 20th-century socialism like public ownership of the means of production and planned economy failed to realize the promise of collective abundance,[52] and this was no exception for Cuba. Socialism requires that the

---

[51] Editors, "Why Fidel Castro's Communism Failed", Live Mint, December 1st, 2016, https://www.livemint.com/Opinion/qOU9bv10JQ4vKu2MzM V82L/Why-Fidel-Castros-communism-failed.html. Article. Web.
[52] Editors, Ibid.

government owns the major inputs to production and to formulate an economy-wide production and distribution plan.[53] Moreover, planning necessarily entails centralizing a great deal of power—the people in power often lack any incentive to plan efficiently even if they knew how to do it.[54] Like the Soviet Union, Cuba has had a centrally-planned economy with a command style. The Cuban command-planning style of Fidel Castro, like that of the Soviet Union, advocated for a directive administrative planning in which directives are passed down from higher authorities (planning agencies) to agents (enterprise managers), who in

---

[53] Powell, Benjamin, "Cuban Socialism Should Die with Castro", Independent Institute, December 5, 2016, http://www.independent.org/news/article.asp?id=8938. Article. Web.
[54] Powell, Ibid.

turn give orders to workers.[55] The economic redistribution in Cuba was, indeed, substantially inadequate. Educated Cuban citizens such as engineers, socialist intellectuals (professors and writers), lawyers and medical doctors have guaranteed jobs within the government while Cubans who are less educated have extremely limited opportunities for their economic and personal growth. The central-planning economy of Cuba determined the fate of its citizens. It entails that, for a Cuban citizen to be economically prosperous, he/she had to conform to the government's requirements by fulfilling a set of formalities that would legitimatize the eligibility of that individual in order to qualify for economic prosperity. Those Cubans with limited education,

---

[55] Wilhelm, John Howard, (1985). "The Soviet Union has an Administered, Not a Planned, Economy". Soviet Studies. 37. (1):118-130

have restricted economic opportunities because the Cuban socialist government is the entity that controlled these economic opportunities. And these less-educated Cubans did not fit into the government's requirements and criteria because they did not have the adequate credentials to be eligible to Cuba's higher society. This system established by the Cuban government has failed the Cuban people, and it has substantiated the hypocrisy and injustice of socialism in Cuba. In the United States for instance, less-educated citizens can still become economically prosperous because the American economic system relies on personal incentives and individual initiative rather than quantification by a central authority. The American economic system which is based on a free-market economy, enlarges the amount of opportunities available to people thank to the expansion of the market. Individuals living under a centrally-planned economy have very limited and restrained economic opportunities, and their living standard is way below the poverty line, compared to countries that have adopted capitalism and a free-market economy. Besides the dissolution of the Soviet Union—Cuba, which has had a centrally-planned economy, is the living proof that epitomizes the failure of socialism in the twentieth and twenty-first centuries.

The third country wherein socialism/communism has deliberately failed, is Vietnam. Vietnam's geographical location was geopolitically and economically paramount for the western world, and particularly for the United States. Geopolitically, Vietnam was an asset for the United States because it was the only country in Southeast Asia that was capitalist before the rise of

Ho Chi Minh. Southeast Asian countries like Laos, Cambodia, Singapore, and Thailand, have already espoused Marxist politics as means of government. Consequently; Vietnam, which was then-colonized by the French government, was the only country that was resisting the implementation of communism in the region. The defeat of the French led the Americans to carry on the mission. That mission was to contain communism in Southeast Asia. It was paramount for the United States that Vietnam does not fall into communism because a communist Vietnam would mean the loss of political and economic influences from the United States in Southeast Asia. The rise of Ho Chi Minh promulgated the division of Vietnam into two antagonistic states: South Vietnam and North Vietnam. South Vietnam, which was subsequently ruled by Bao Dai, Ngo Dinh Nhu, Nguyen Văn

Thieu, and Trân Vān Hu'o'ng; was economically capitalistic and open to a free-market economy. It was vividly supported by the United States and the majority of western countries. North Vietnam, on the other hand, was ruled by communist leader Ho Chi Minh, who was supported by the Soviet Union, The People's Republic of China, and the Socialist Republic of India. The Vietnam War, which lasted twenty years (1955-1975), ended with the victory of North Vietnam over South Vietnam; therefore, the prevalence of socialism and Marxism over capitalism in Southeast Asia. The unification of Vietnam has established Marxism as its principal political regime. Vietnam has, evidently, given way to a centralized economy as in the other two countries (Soviet Union and Cuba) previously mentioned. The Vietnamese economy struggled from the very commencement of its unification. As a matter of fact, the United States went on to demand that the Vietnamese communist government repays millions of dollars borrowed by its enemy, the old Saigon regime.[56] Vietnam desperately needed the world to provide trades and aid that could turn its economy around.[57] Although Vietnam had a centralized economy, its style was, however, different from the strict Soviet command-style. The Vietnamese socialist government followed the Chinese model of central-planning economy. This Chinese central-planning economy, which was, nonetheless, a planned economy—did not play an operational role in the allocation of resources among

---

[56] Davies, Nick, "Vietnam 40 Years on: How a Communist Victory gave way to capitalist corruption", The Guardian, April 22, 2015, https://www.theguardian.com/news/2015/apr/22/vietnam-40-years-on-how-communist-victory-gave-way-to-capitalist-corruption. Article. Web.
[57] Ibid.

productive units in the economy[58] unlike that of the Soviet Union. This economic system has allowed Vietnam to be economically sustained for a while. Indeed, from 1991 to 2010, Vietnam achieved a steady annual GDP growth rate of 7.7 percent,[59] which reduced the poverty level from 58 percent to 10 percent.[60] However, this economic prosperity was not long-lasting. After a period of steady growth, Vietnam is now standing at a critical crossroad as the effects of an endless economic crisis worldwide and an overheating economy.[61] The Vietnamese economic growth has been slowing down since the

---

[58] Dowlah, Abu F. (1992). "Theoretical Expositions of Centralized versus Decentralized Strands of Socialist Economic Systems", International Journal of Social Economics. Emerald.19 (7/8/9)210-258.

[59] Truong, Quang, "Time To Rethink Vietnam's Socialist Principles", East Asia Forum, December 4, 2013. http://www.eastasiaforum.org/2013/12/04/time-to-rethink-vietnams-socialist-principles/. Article. Web.

[60] Truong, Ibid.

[61] Truong, Ibid.

global financial crisis, and corruption as a result of "capitalist cronyism" and related vested interested has become rampant, especially in state-owned sector.[62] Furthermore, the living conditions of the people have worsened through soaring inflation due to a lack of consistent monetary policies and poor governance.[63] The Vietnamese failed-system needs a comprehensive and a set of safe solutions to prevent total collapse.[64] This example illustrates that socialism has also failed in Vietnam.

I used these three countries (Soviet Union, Cuba, and Vietnam) to corroborate the failure of socialism as an economic system and as a political regime. I chose these three countries because they all played a fundamental role in world politics. The Soviet Union was the hope of a serious alternative to

---

[62] Truong, Ibid.
[63] Truong, Ibid.
[64] Truong, Ibid.

capitalism worldwide. Cuba and Vietnam played that same role in their respective geographical regions. These three countries economically failed because they all had a centralized economy. I have reiterated in the previous chapter that a government with a centralized economy has no choice but to use coercion to impose equality. The example of these three countries is characterized by the precept that equality of outcome is inherently flawed because it is opposed to the fundamental principles of human nature. These three examples clearly exhibited the fact that government is not the right entity to convey economic prosperity. Socialism has failed in these three countries, and it is a clear fact. Democratic socialism is absolutely no different from classical socialism. The reason why they are both similar is because they both rely on coercion and arbitrary rule to achieve equality. A democratic socialist government if implemented at first, would use "democratic" means to achieve results, as it is stated in its definition. But these democratic means will be short-lasting because in order to exercise control over the means of production, and in order to uphold an egalitarian society, the use of coercion (in all sense of the word) will be a principal instrument to convey government policy. It implies that a democratic socialist government will increasingly and substantially become authoritarian as it pursues its egalitarian policies. It will legitimize compulsion as the thread to justify its political action. It will pass laws that will constrain individual's freedom to a very limited set of choices as it was the case of socialism in Cuba and in the Soviet Union. The worst of all is that a democratic socialist government will progressively eradicate our constitutional rights.

Democratic socialism in its core, is the greatest

fallacy in contemporary politics.

References

Polychroniou, C J, "The Failed Dream of a Russian Revolution" Aljazeera, October 25, 2017, https://www.aljazeera.com/indepth/opinion/failed-dream-russian-revolution-171018082225358.html. Article. Web.

Gregory, Paul R. "Why Socialism Fails", Defining Ideas, Hoover Institution Journal, The Hoover Institution, January 10, 2018, https://www.hoover.org/research/why-socialism-fails. Article. Web.

Gregory, Ibid.

Gregory, Ibid.

Gregory and Stuart, Comparing Economic System in the Twenty-First Century, 2003. ISBN 0-618-26181-8. P.127.

Gregory, Paul R. "Why Socialism Fails", Defining Ideas, Hoover Institution Journal, The Hoover Institution, January 10, 2018, https://www.hoover.org/research/why-socialism-fails. Article. Web.

Gregory, Ibid.

Gregory, Ibid.

Palmer, Tom G. "Why Socialism Collapsed in Eastern Europe", Cato Institute, October 1990, https://www.cato.org/publications/commentary/why-socialism-collapsed-eastern-europe. Article, Web.

Palmer, Ibid.

Palmer, Ibid.

Palmer, Ibid.

Palmer, Ibid.

Wikipedia Contributors, "Fidel Castro", Wikipedia, the Free Encyclopedia, November 2018, web.
Marsh, Sarah, "Cuba Aims to Build Socialism, Not Communism, In Draft Constitution", Reuters, July 21, 2018, https://www.reuters.com/article/us-cuba-assembly/cuba-aims-to-build-socialism-not-communism-in-draft-constitution-idUSKBN1KB0ML. Article. Web.

Wikipedia Contributors, Ibid.

Editors, "Cuba Aims For Socialism, Not Communism", The Sydney Morning Herald, July 22, 2018, https://www.smh.com.au/world/central-america/cuba-aims-for-socialism-not-communism-20180722-p4zsw5.html. Article. Web.

Editors, Ibid.

McRae, Hamish, "Fidel Castro's Cuba Failed Economically-But He Had Little Choice In The Matter", Independent, November 26, 2017, https://www.independent.co.uk/voices/fidel-castro-economy-death-cuba-economics-communism-a7441066.html. Article. Web.

McRae, Ibid.

McRae, Ibid.

McRae, Ibid.

McRae, Ibid.

Editors, "Why Fidel Castro's Communism Failed", Live Mint, December 1st, 2016,

https://www.livemint.com/Opinion/qOU9bv10JQ4v
Ku2MzMV82L/Why-Fidel-Castros-communism-
failed.html. Article. Web.

Editors, Ibid.

Powell, Benjamin, "Cuban Socialism Should Die
with Castro", Independent Institute, December 5,
2016,
http://www.independent.org/news/article.asp?id=8
938. Article. Web.

Powell, Ibid.

Wilhelm, John Howard, (1985). "The Soviet Union
has an Administered, Not a Planned, Economy".
Soviet Studies. 37. (1):118-130
Davies, Nick, "Vietnam 40 Years on: How a
Communist Victory gave way to capitalist
corruption", The Guardian, April 22, 2015,
https://www.theguardian.com/news/2015/apr/22/vi
etnam-40-years-on-how-communist-victory-gave-
way-to-capitalist-corruption. Article. Web.

Davies, Ibid.

Dowlah, Abu F. (1992). "Theoretical Expositions of Centralized versus Decentralized Strands of Socialist Economic Systems", International Journal of Social Economics. Emerald.19 (7/8/9)210-258.

Truong, Quang, "Time To Rethink Vietnam's Socialist Principles", East Asia Forum, December 4, 2013.
http://www.eastasiaforum.org/2013/12/04/time-to-rethink-vietnams-socialist-principles/. Article. Web.

Truong, Ibid.

Truong, Ibid.

Truong, Ibid.

Truong, Ibid.

Truong, Ibid.

FOUR

COMMUNISM:
THE LOGICAL FALLACY
OF KARL MARX

Karl Marx was undeniably one of the greatest political philosophers of all times. His thoughts have transformed nations and, to this day, have had a substantial influence on the generations of the twentieth century and those of the post-Soviet era. His thinking and writings have become a political doctrine taught in the most prestigious academic institutions in the world.

It is certainly irrefutable that Karl Marx, as a thinker, writer, and philosopher; has dearly contributed to the development of modern political philosophy. His contribution has advanced the expansion of the system of ideas. However, Karl Marx unwittingly developed, through his writings, the deadliest and most fallacious ideology of all the political thoughts that could ever exist in the history of humanity. This lethal ideology was communism and it is, up to today, the greatest logical and political fallacy of the twentieth century.

The Roots of Communism

Communism, based on the *Merriam-Webster Dictionary*, is a political ideology that advocated for a system in which goods are owned in common and are available to all as needed.[65] Like socialism, Communism is an economic and political structure that promotes equality and seeks to eliminate social classes.[66] While living in England, Marx and Engels observed that the workers were unfairly treated by their employers and unjustly remunerated for their labor. Workers were working tirelessly for long

---

[65] "Communism" *Merriam-Webster Dictionary* (2019).

[66] Editor, "The Difference Between Communism and Socialism," *Investopedia,* (2018).

96

hours and gained wages that were below the level of subsistence. The horrible living conditions of the working-class in England incentivized Marx's friend and collaborator, Friedrich Engels, to publish in 1845 this book entitled *The Condition of the Working Class in England.* This book was, indeed, the groundwork of what is going to become the *Communist Manifesto.* Marx observed that the condition of the working-class in England was not only limited to English society. The appalled details of the conditions under which the working-class had to go through were the same all over Europe. The industrialists, those who held the means of production, had control over the resources needed to produce capital. The worker produced the capital and the industrialists retained the profit of that capital produced; which in return, left the worker with nothing. For Marx, the condition of the worker and that of the working-class, was an injustice that needed to be rectified. In 1848, he and Engels published the most revolutionary book of all times, which would serve as a social remedy to the working-class, to the disenfranchised and the most vulnerable members of society. This book was a political pamphlet entitled *The Communist Manifesto*. Henceforth, *The Communist Manifesto* had become the holy book of the working-class all around the world. It was the book of reference that every worker shall read in order to be enlightened and emancipated. In the book, Marx draws up the ideas that would theoretically set the worker free. Marx had centered communism on three principles: Equality, Freedom and Justice.

Equality is the first principle because the ultimate goal of communism was to achieve a classless society in which everyone would be equal to one another. Marx and Engels thought of the proletariat as the group of individuals with labor power, and the bourgeoisie as those who own the means of production in a capitalist society.[67] Marx professed that the surest way to achieve equality in a communist society was to abolish private ownership so that the means of production would belong to the entire community[68] rather than to specific individuals. For Marx, the quest for equality was social equality. For Marx, equality was not to be confused with the uniformity of laws, as understood by liberal ideology.[69] The abolition of private

---

[67] "History and Background of Communism: Foundation, Goals, and Priorities." *Communism and Computer Ethics.*https://cs.stanford.edu/people/eroberts/cs181/projects/2007-08/communism-computing-china/index.html. Article. Web.

[68] *Ibid.*

[69] Pereira, Potyara, "The Concept of Equality and Well-Being in Marx," *Thematic Space: Marx, Marxism and Social Work Essay.* (2013). Revista Katalysis Vol. 16 No.1. Florianopolis. ISSN 1982-

property would promulgate the abolition of social classes. A classless society would ensure that all humans are equal in their self-righteousness, and that they would have access to all available opportunities.

The second principle of communism is liberty. On that note, Marx believed that if the state was the regulator of public ownership, all individuals would be free to have access to public goods since common property suggests that it belongs to everyone. Under the concept of common ownership theoretically, the worker would enjoy the production of his labor because he will be the owner of that production. Labor power is the worker's

---

0259. http://www.scielo.br/scielo.php?pid=S1414-49802013000100005&script=sci_arttext&tlng=en. Article.

capacity to produce goods and services.[70] Marx wrongly dismissed the contribution that business owners bring into the production of goods and services; and he maintained that the capitalist business owner was exploiting the labor of the worker. Therefore, it is time for the trend to be reversed and for the proletariat to govern society. A classless society in which the production of goods and services are all managed by the state rather than by individuals, would enable that production to be redistributed adequately.

The third principle of communism is justice. As justice is being an essentially distributive value, it is argued that, furthermore, to attribute to Marx a concern with justice is to inflect his critique of

---

[70] Prychitko, David, *Marxism*, The Library of Economics and Liberty. https://www.econlib.org/library/Enc/Marxism.html. Article. Web.

capitalism in a direction he explicitly repudiated.[71]
Marx's conception of justice is actually social justice.
Communism advocates for an equal redistribution
of wealth and opportunity. It especially gives
privileges to members of the proletariat. In a
communist society, every person will be entitled to
a fair judicial system in which discrimination will be
attenuated and eradicated. Marx offered to
humanity a utopian society in which equality,
freedom, and justice would prevail as the guardians
of a just society. For Marx, socialism and
communism were the next logical steps following
the collapse of capitalism. Capitalism was a mere
ephemeral situation that was adjusted to the human

---

[71] Geras, Norman, "Reformist" *The Controversy About Marx and Justice,* From Marxist Theory, Ed. A. Callinicos, OUP (1989). https://www.marxists.org/reference/subject/philosophy/works/us/geras.htm. Article. Web.

condition at a given time. Marx projected that communism would be the ultimate purpose to achieve in order to obtain a just society.

Communism in Practice

Communism, in practice, was very far different than what Marx envisioned in his book. In fact, communism has failed miserably in every country in which it was implemented. Communism is the easiest system to sell to people who are poor, not because poor people are stupid or lazy or envious of partaking in banquets of the rich, but because communist and socialist rhetoric sound so reasonable, fair and workable.[72] The first country on

---

[72] Editor, *Why Communism Always Fails? – Kept Simple for The General Reader.* News 24. (2014). https://www.news24.com/MyNews24/Why-Communism-

earth to have applied communism as a political and economic system was Soviet Russia in 1917 after the Bolshevik Revolution. The most important fact to understand about the economics of communism is that communist revolutions triumphed only in heavily agricultural societies.[73] Government ownership of the means of production could not, therefore, be achieved by expropriating a few industrialists.[74] Lenin recognized that the government would have to seize the lands of tens of millions of peasants, who surely would resist.[75] Lenin attempted to seize these lands during the

ALWAYS-fails-kept-simple-for-the-general-reader-20140826.
Article. Web.

[73] Caplan, Bryan, *Communism*, The Library of Economics and Liberty,
https://www.econlib.org/library/Enc/Communism.html.
Article. Web.

[74] *Ibid.*

[75] *Ibid.*

Russian Civil War (1918-1920), but retreated in the face of chaos and five million famine deaths.[76] Lenin's successor, Joseph Stalin, finished the job a decade later, sending millions of more affluent peasants to Siberian slave labor camps also known as the Gulag to forestall organized resistance and starving into submission.[77] The collectivization of the means of production empowered the state to arbitrarily deprive individuals of the production of their labor. Contrary to capitalism; in communism, the worker was coerced by the state to forsake the profit of what he has worked for and produced. It is interesting to witness how hypocritical the ideology that advocated for the freedom of the worker is the very same ideology that enslaved the worker to even

---

[76] *Ibid.*

[77] *Ibid.*

worst conditions than what they were subjected to in England during the nineteenth century. At least in England, workers were not interned into concentration camps like in Soviet Russia or in China.

Communism in Soviet Russia was the reflection of an oppressive, tyrannical, and arbitrary form of government. Three years after the Russian Revolution, an Austrian economist, Ludwig von Mises, wrote in 1920 that communism or socialism could not succeed because it had abolished the free-market so that officials had no market prices to guide them in planning production.[78] Planning was to be done by a central committee, insuring plenty for everyone.[79] As Mises pointed out, the raw materials,

---

[78] Bettina Bien Greaves, *Why Communism Failed*, Foundation for Economic Education. (1991). https://fee.org/articles/why-communism-failed/. Article. Web.

[79] *Ibid.*

labor, tools, and machines used in socialist production are outside the market—they are owned by government and controlled by government planners.[80] No one can buy them or sell them, no market price can develop for them because they are not exchangeable.[81] Communism failed in the Soviet Union as well as in Eastern Europe because central planners did not know the relative values—the exchange ratios or market prices of the countless factors of production involved.[82] Without market prices, the planners have no clues as to the relative values of iron, aluminum, lumber, the new synthetics, or railroads, oil fields, farm lands, power

---

[80] *Ibid.*

[81] *Ibid.*

[82] *Ibid.*

plants, bridges, or housing.[83] Without market prices for the factors of production, the planners are at a loss as to how to coordinate and channel production to satisfy the most urgent needs of consumers. Communism; whether it was in the Soviet Union, Eastern Europe, China, Angola, Cuba, North Korea, or Vietnam; has failed because a centralized economy does not comprehend market prices and the other signals that an economy needs to enhance growth. The state kept spending money without calculating the monetary value of the material being produced. Communism or socialism; wherever it was effectuated; generated oppressive governments, centralized economies, and the enslavement of individual. Lenin, Stalin, Mao Zedong, Pol Pot, Castro, Ceausescu, Dos Santos, Kim-Il-Sung; all these communist leaders have enslaved and

---

[83] *Ibid.*

108

slaughtered millions of their fellow countrymen in order to ascertain their power. They have done so in the name of socialism, communism, equality, justice, and prosperity.

What Did Marx Get Wrong About Communism?

Karl Marx, in formulating his political thoughts on communism, had certainly not envisioned that his theories would take such a turn. He surely did not anticipate that, what he thought that would bring salvation to the working-class, was in reality a civil genocide, a carnage of civilian populations. Marxist and socialist intellectuals have attempted to save Marx's reputation by claiming that Marx had been misunderstood. They even furthered their claims by avowing that the communism that took place in the Soviet Union,

China, or Cuba; was a perversion of Marx's thought, and not what Marx had truly foreseen.

The truth is that Marx was not misunderstood. He is the one who miscomprehended communism. Communism is a fundamentally erroneous ideology for the simple reason that it is contrary to human nature. Man is above all an individual, and the highest moral purpose of an individual is happiness. Happiness can be interpreted as the freedom of oneself to pursue his own self-interests. As an individual, it is in the nature of man to keep the benefits of what he produces for himself because profit is what maintains the self-preservation of the individual and incentivizes him to achieve higher purposes. Human beings are flawed beings. It is because they are imperfect that they have created a system of government that would have limited powers. A

110

government that would be strong enough to protect and preserve their natural rights but not excessively mighty to tyrannize them. In his conception of a communist society, Marx gave a central role to the state. For Marx, the state is the one that will free the worker from the subjugation of capitalism. Since private property is abolished in a communist society and everything belonged to the state under the symbol of collectivization and public ownership; Marx has, yet, forgotten or miscalculated that the state is an organization run by imperfect beings who are primarily stimulated by their own self-interests rather than promulgating the common good. Hence, it is unsurprising to see that all communist leaders were evidently despotic and oppressive leaders.

By collectivizing the production of the workers, those who rule the state are those who benefit from the workers' production. If the state is

the sole beneficiary and guarantor of the workers'
production, then to whom the workers will
complain to if they are underpaid or if their labor
rights are violated? Who will repair the injustice
against the state if the state is the one who has the
monopoly of justice? Marx did surely not think that
far ahead. He was mostly blinded by this utopia and
was, thus, persuaded that it would work but he was
definitely wrong. Communism has created more
inequalities in communist countries than capitalism
has done so in capitalist societies because the state
deprived man from pursuing his own self-interests.
That being said, communism is a logical and
political fallacy.

References

"Communism" Merriam-Webster Dictionary (2019).

Editor, "The Difference Between Communism and Socialism," Investopedia, (2018).

"History and Background of Communism: Foundation, Goals, and Priorities." Communism andComputer Ethics.https://cs.stanford.edu/people/eroberts/cs181/projects/2007-08/communism-computing-china/index.html. Article. Web.

Ibid.

Pereira, Potyara, "The Concept of Equality and Well-Being in Marx," Thematic Space: Marx, Marxism and Social Work Essay. (2013). Revista Katalysis Vol. 16 No.1. Florianopolis. ISSN 1982-0259. http://www.scielo.br/scielo.php?pid=S1414-49802013000100005&script=sci_arttext&tlng=en. Article.

Prychitko, David, Marxism, The Library of Economics and Liberty. https://www.econlib.org/library/Enc/Marxism.html. Article. Web.

Geras, Norman, "Reformist" The Controversy About Marx and Justice, From Marxist Theory, Ed. A. Callinicos, OUP (1989). https://www.marxists.org/reference/subject/philosophy/works/us/geras.htm. Article. Web.

Editor, Why Communism Always Fails? – Kept Simple for The General Reader. News 24. (2014). https://www.news24.com/MyNews24/Why-Communism-ALWAYS-fails-kept-simple-for-the-general-reader-20140826. Article. Web.

Caplan, Bryan, Communism, The Library of Economics and Liberty, https://www.econlib.org/library/Enc/Communism.html. Article. Web.

Ibid.

Ibid.

Ibid.

Ibid.

Bettina Bien Greaves, Why Communism Failed, Foundation for Economic Education. (1991). https://fee.org/articles/why-communism-failed/. Article. Web.

Ibid.

Ibid.

Ibid.

Ibid.

Ibid.

PART TWO

DEMOCRATIC SOCIALISM IN AMERICA:

WHY IT WON'T WORK

FIVE

The Roots of Libertarianism and Egalitarianism in America

The Constitution of the United States, which was drafted in 1787-1788 and enforced in 1789, was based upon a very fundamental question: How much power should the government exercise over the people? This question has been the foundational and perpetual debate between the Hamiltonians and the Jeffersonians. A precept whereupon both schools of thought agreed upon was that, civil society must be rooted in the principles of liberty. The elemental disagreement between the two schools was based on the role of government in a free society. How much is government needed to ensure liberty?

The Hamiltonians, also known as the Federalists, believed that a strong central government was the necessary entity to ensure life, liberty, property, and the pursuit of happiness. The Hamiltonians advocated for broad constitutional powers for the federal government, including national defense and finance.[84] According to Alexander Hamilton and the Federalists, a lesser degree of individual liberties and civic rights would follow federal powers.[85] The Hamiltonians furthered their economic stances on the premise that government intervention is, and should be the mandatory and indispensable expedient to regulate the economy. When Alexander Hamilton became the first United States Secretary of Treasury within the new federal government, he developed a substantial fiscal and economic system based on a national coinage, a national banking system, a revenue program to provide for the repayment of the national debt, and measures to encourage

---

[84] Editors, "Alexander Hamilton", *West's Encyclopedia of American Law* (2005), The Gale Group Inc., https://www.encyclopedia.com/people/history/us-history-biographies/alexander-hamilton. Article. Web.
[85] Editors, Ibid.

industrial and commercial development.[86] The Hamiltonian economic program conceptualized its economic system on economic nationalism. Economic nationalism signifies that the central government plays an extensive role within economic regulation. Alexander Hamilton's economic policy was mainly focused on four central elements which are the foreign debt, the national debt, the debts of the States, and the system of taxation. Firstly, on the foreign debt, Hamilton proposed that the federal government pays the interest out of tax revenues and borrows over a fifteen-year period, enough capital to repay the principal of loans.[87] This policy granted the government to be sole grantor regarding

---

[86] Editors, Ibid.

[87] Editors, "Hamilton's Economic Policies", *Dictionary of American History*, (2003), The Gale Group Inc. https://www.encyclopedia.com/history/dictionaries-thesauruses-pictures-and-press-releases/hamiltons-economic-policies. Article. Web.

the reimbursement of foreign debts. Hamilton was absolutely right on the question of the foreign debts. Since the federal government is the entity that has the power to protect the rights of its citizens, and the duty to protect the national interest against all foreign threats or coercion, it is, thus, the role of the federal government to repay the foreign debt of the United States. Secondly, on the national debt's question, Alexander Hamilton recommended a "redemption of the debt at full value" to repay the debts that the Continental Congress and the Confederation government had incurred by borrowing domestically.[88] By redemption, he [Hamilton] meant offering to trade the complicated morass of notes and bonds of varying durations and interest rates for new, long-term federal bonds.[89]

---

[88] Editors, Ibid.
[89] Editors, Ibid.

Hamilton recommended that the federal government maintains this new debt as a permanent feature of the fiscal landscape. In order to sustain the new national debts, the Treasury would establish a fund within a national bank and supply it with surplus revenues of the post and proceeds of a new European loan.[90] The creation of the new national debt through the national bank, enabled the federal government to regulate the means of production in order to stabilize the national economy. Thirdly, on the debts of the States, Hamilton proposed that the federal government would take over the $25 million in debt that state governments had accumulated during the Revolution.[91] The policy of the debts of the States was called the "assumption program." By implementing this program, Hamilton sought to

---

[90] Editors, Ibid.
[91] Editors, Ibid.

strengthen further the nation's financial reputation, to bolster the nation's stock of capital, and to enhance the financial power of the federal government.[92] Fourth and lastly, on taxation, Alexander Hamilton proposed a tariff law. This tariff law or tax law was designed to raise revenues for the new government.[93] The law established a complex set of duties on imports, rebates for re-exported goods, and special favors for imports carried in American vessels.[94] The tax law system invigorated by Hamilton, legitimized the financial power of the federal government over state and local taxation. It asserted the control of the federal government over state and local taxation system. To an extent, the federal government system of taxation was intended to subdue state and local taxations.

---

[92] Editors, Ibid.
[93] Editors, Ibid.
[94] Editors, Ibid.

The taxation that each citizen had to pay to the federal government was twice of that he or she had to pay to its local and state governments. The Constitution of the United States provided substantial political and economic power to the federal government through Hamiltonian philosophy. The Hamiltonian political philosophy advocates for a more or less centralized economic system, in which the federal government is the principal administrator of this economy. The Hamiltonians championed a political economy in which government intervention would certainly be maximized but not absolute, because an absolute government intervention into the economy would inevitably lead to the tyranny of the federal government. In short, it is fair to say that the Hamiltonians are proponents of Keynesian Economics. Overall, the economic policy of the

Hamiltonians was meant to promulgate the expansion of federal authority.

On the other hand, the Jeffersonians; also known as the Anti-Federalists, strongly maintained that a limited government is the real entity that secures the life, liberty, property, and the pursuit of happiness of the citizen. The Jeffersonians advocated for a restricted and limited constitutional power of the central government. They believed that government is effective when it plays a minimal role within the economy. Thomas Jefferson is very well-known for being the ideological adversary of Alexander Hamilton. To counter Hamilton's ideas of having a constitution that would give full power to the central government, Thomas Jefferson, with many other Anti-Federalists such as George Mason, Samuel Adams or Robert Yates; incorporated the Bill of Rights in the Constitution in order to bring a balance of power between the citizenry and the central government. Since the essence of American civil society is founded on freedom, the Bill of Rights is, thus, the guarantor of individual liberties. Jefferson asserted that the central and fundamental role of the federal government is nothing more than to protect and secure the rights and property of the people. This philosophy of human nature, which preaches individual liberty according to Jefferson, is also conformed with his economic philosophy. Thomas Jefferson was a proponent of a decentralized economy. The third President of the United States [Jefferson] adopted the view that the federal government should be frugal in their expenses and not cause a large amount of taxation on the business owner, or the farmers toiling in the fields.[95]   It is important to comprehend that the economic vision of Thomas Jefferson is grounded in promulgating liberty. He, therefore, enhanced a limited intervention of the government in the economy. Jeffersonian's economic conceptualization was based on an agrarian and pastoral society. Jefferson believed that government should not interfere with agriculture but should let it develop in its own way, which he thought would be in the form of independent homesteads.[96] He was opposed to state's offering ways of manufacturing, was also opposed to America's becoming involved in an

---

[95] Franz, Joel, "Thomas Jefferson and Economic Policy" (2016), https://buzzazz.com/advertising-and-marketing/politics/jeffersonthomas-jefferson-and-economic-policy/. Article. Web.

[96] Grampp, William, "Jefferson's Economics", *Early Republican Economic Policy*, Economic Liberalism, Vol.1 *The Beginnings*, Online Library of Liberty, (1965), https://oll.libertyfund.org/pages/early-republican-economic-policy. Article. Web.

extensive foreign trade and believed that what little trade was necessary should be conducted with entire freedom.[97] In his second term as President, Thomas Jefferson still relied on agriculture, but now favored more production for the market including the foreign market.[98] In his foreign trade policy, Jefferson urged a program of reciprocity in which the United States would trade freely with those countries that traded freely with it and would restrict its trade with others.[99] The choice to restrict foreign trades would limit the economic power of the federal government strictly to the national interests of the United States. Furthermore, the Jeffersonians vehemently opposed the "assumption program" of the Hamiltonians, which dealt with the debts of the States. In fact, they believed that the

---

[97] Grampo, Ibid.
[98] Grampo, Ibid.
[99] Grampo, Ibid.

assumption program promoted by the Hamiltonians was an economic method to expand federal authority over state and local sovereignty. That being said, the Jeffersonians asseverated that manufacturing should be encouraged by state and local governments because it could be conducted on a smaller scale, preferably on farms as household manufacturing.[100] The fundamental ideal of the Jeffersonian agricultural economy was entrenched within a collection of self-sufficient homesteads on each of which there were household manufactures.[101] It implied a collection of independent and economically isolated farms, on each of which the dwellers consumed only what they produced.[102] The agricultural economy of Thomas Jefferson favored a form of liberalism

---

[100] Grampo, Ibid.
[101] Grampo, Ibid.
[102] Grampo, Ibid.

within the economy. Its reliance on self-sufficient incentives stimulated a free-market approach to the economic system. Thomas Jefferson held that a free-market economic system enforces the principle of the freedom to choose. The more the economic system is decentralized, which means the government plays a less controlling role in the market, the greater the people, who are private actors in the market, have a larger set of options upon how they want to conduct their own economic endeavors. Under free-market economics, the people are free to make their decisions as to the numbers of a product that are necessary from one day to the next.[103] Jefferson has comprehended that private ownership is the indispensable vector that

---

[103] Editors, "Allowing People To Decide or Decentralized Planning", *Free Market Economics*, December 2011, The Thomas Jefferson Center For Constitutional Restoration. https://thomasjeffersoncenter.com/2011/12/02/free-market-economics/. Article. Web.

stimulates the functioning of a free-market economy. The Bill of Rights, which protects the unalienable rights of the citizens, has allowed the free-market economic system to not only benefit the citizens of the United States but the population of the entire world.[104] Adjunctively, the Jeffersonians championed the price system under a free-market economy. The price system under free-market economics determines the overall numbers of products that are available for the consumer.[105] The people decide what products will or will not be produced and in what quantities the products will be produced.[106] All things considered, the Jeffersonians articulated that a limited government, a government with limited power to shape the economy, is imperative to prompt economic

---

[104] Editors, Ibid.
[105] Editors, Ibid.
[106] Editors, Ibid.

incentives within a free society. If the people are free, they should, therefore, be free to control and conduct their own means of production. Since the citizens are taxpayers, they pay the government so that the latter in return will secure their rights and liberty. Jeffersonian philosophy believes in a market-control economy rather than government-control. Capitalism and liberty are its driving force.

The ideological contention between Hamiltonians and Jeffersonians on the role of the federal government within the economy, has succinctly engendered two antagonistic doctrines that separate the American people on societal issues. These two antagonistic principles are libertarianism and egalitarianism. Before debating on the substance of the two doctrines, it is, first and foremost, quintessential to remember that the American society was founded on liberty. The Founding

Fathers to the Constitution of the United States wanted a government that would be strong enough to ensure the security of the citizens' rights, but also wanted a government with limited powers to prevent it from sinking into tyranny. The Founding Fathers have, thus, created a constitution that would prevail individual liberty over political power. Now that the clarification regarding the philosophical nature of the political culture of the United States has been ascertained, let's get into the bottom of these two adversarial doctrines that defined the American republic.

Libertarianism is a political philosophy that takes liberty to be the primary political value.[107] According to David Boaz, the Executive Vice President of the Cato Institute and conspicuous

---

[107] Boaz, David, "Libertarianism", *Encyclopedia Britannica, Politics.* https://www.britannica.com/topic/libertarianism-politics. Article. Web.

libertarian thinker, libertarianism is encapsulated into nine key concepts. The first, and unequivocal concept of libertarianism is individualism. Libertarians perceive the individual as the basic unit of social analysis—only individuals make choices and are responsible for their actions.[108] The libertarian thought emphasizes on the dignity of each individual, which entails both rights and responsibility.[109] The second concept of Libertarianism is entrenched in individual rights. Proponents of libertarianism maintain that individuals are primarily moral agents. Because individuals are moral agents, they have a right to be secured in their life, liberty, and property.[110] These

---

[108] Boaz, David, "Key Concepts of Libertarianism", *Libertarianism: A Primer*, Cato Institute, January 1, 1999, https://www.cato.org/publications/commentary/key-concepts-libertarianism. Article. Web.
[109] Boaz, Ibid.
[110] Boaz, Ibid.

unalienable rights are not granted by government or by society; they are inherent in the nature of human beings.[111] The third concept of libertarianism is the Spontaneous Order. The spontaneous order reflects the asserted authority. The great insight of libertarian social analysis is that order in society arises spontaneously, out of the actions of thousands or millions of individuals who coordinate their actions with those of others in order to achieve their purposes.[112] The fourth concept of libertarianism is the belief in the Rule of Law. The advocates of libertarianism staunchly believe that a society functions under better conditions when it is regulated by the law. Individuals are free to pursue their own lives so long as they respect the equal rights of others.[113] The rule of law means that

---

[111] Boaz, Ibid.
[112] Boaz, Ibid.
[113] Boaz, Ibid.

individuals are governed by generally applicable and spontaneous developed legal rules, not by arbitrary commands; and those rules should protect the freedom of individuals to pursue happiness in their own ways.[114] The fifth element of libertarianism is determined in its belief in a limited government. Limited government is the basic political implication of libertarianism—they want to divide and limit power, and that means specially to limit government through a written constitution enumerating and limiting the powers that the people delegate to government.[115] The sixth component that ascertains libertarianism is free-market economics. For libertarians, a free-market economy is the economic driving force of a free society. The right to property entails the right to exchange property by mutual

---

[114] Boaz, Ibid.
[115] Boaz, Ibid.

agreement.[116] Libertarians believe that people will be both freer and more prosperous if government intervention in people's economic choices is minimized.[117] The seventh concept of libertarianism is the Virtue of Production. Libertarians defended the right of people to keep the fruits of their labor,[118] which is, indeed, the virtue of the free-market. The virtue of production is developed into a respect for the dignity of work and production and especially for the growing middle-class, who were looked down upon by aristocrats.[119] The eighth concept of libertarian thought is expressed in the Natural Harmony of Interests. Libertarianism stipulates that there is a natural harmony of interests among peaceful, productive people in a just society.[120]

---

[116] Boaz, Ibid.
[117] Boaz, Ibid.
[118] Boaz, Ibid.
[119] Boaz, Ibid.
[120] Boaz, Ibid.

Furthermore, libertarianism advocates that the free-market allows the conveyance of peaceful and harmonious self-interests. Only when government begins to hand out rewards on the basis of political pressure do we find ourselves involved in group conflict, pushed to organize and contend with other groups for a piece of political power.[121] Lastly, the ninth concept of libertarianism is peace. Libertarianism is opposed to the conceptualization of war. Free men and women, of course, have often had to defend their own societies against threats; but throughout history, war has usually been the common enemy of peaceful, productive people on all sides of the conflict.[122] A society founded on liberty believes in one form of equality, which is the concept of equality of opportunity. According to

---

[121] Boaz, Ibid.
[122] Boaz, Ibid.

Milton Friedman, the greatest American economist of the second half of the twentieth century; equality of opportunity should contain no arbitrary obstacles placed to prevent individuals from achieving those careers, those positions and those opportunities for which they have the ability, the capacity and taste to qualify.[123] Professor Friedman furthered his explanation by stating that the opportunity should be there for everyone but the person with the most capability should be paid more than the other person with less capability.[124] The substantial value of the concept of equality of opportunity is that it determines an unequal redistribution of wealth. The unequal redistribution of wealth in a free society is legitimate and justified because it is the reward of

---

[123] Friedman, Milton, "Understanding of Equality of Opportunity by Milton Friedman", *Equality and Freedom*, http://www.econ2u.com/friedman/understanding-of-equality-of-opportunity-by-milton-friedman. Lecture. Video.
[124] Friedman, Ibid.

individual labor. The fundamental concept of equality of opportunity measures the value of the individual by his skills and abilities, and not by his identity or other exogenous factors. For instance, we can surely expect two individuals to compete for the same job, which exemplify the opportunity they both have to demonstrate that they are worthy of the task. Evidently, these two individuals competing for the same job will not obtain the same reward. One will obtain a better reward than the other because the one who acquired that reward outperformed his opponent or competitor. This case clearly shows the unequal redistribution of assets or wealth.

On the other hand, egalitarianism in American society, which was originally formulated by the Hamiltonian philosophy on human nature, advocates for a central authority to redistribute wealth. Egalitarianism etymologically, tends to rest on a background idea that all human persons are equal in fundamental worth or moral status.[125] The United States has become an egalitarian society on the political aspect. Political egalitarianism is the pillar of representative government within a multi-ethnic society. Cultural pluralism or societal pluralism is the reflection of different communities that live together under the same set of rules. Political egalitarianism argues that members of society are of equal standing in terms of political power and influence. James Madison for instance, was a proponent of political egalitarianism. Political egalitarianism is, evidently, an asset to our representative government because it supports the principle that every individual is equal under the law. Therefore, the law enables individuals of

---

[125] Editors, "Egalitarianism", *Stanford Encyclopedia of Philosophy,* First published in August 2002; substantive revision in April 2013. https://plato.stanford.edu/entries/egalitarianism/. Web.

difference cultural background to represent their community's interests in government. However, what is not an asset to American society is economic egalitarianism. Indeed, the Hamiltonian philosophy, which advocates for economic egalitarianism, defends the principle that government is the entity that allows equitable redistribution of wealth. The pursuit of equal redistribution of wealth seeks to guarantee the equality of outcome. The Hamiltonian philosophy articulates that government intervention within the economy provides equal redistribution. The problem with equality of outcome is that it subverts liberty. When a society aims to achieve economic egalitarianism, it must subvert liberty. But undermining liberty is uncompromisingly contrary to American constitutional principles of liberty. If the Constitution, which has been fashioned by a limited government in order to preserve liberty, is indeed the engine and the essence of the American political culture, then the will to implement economic equality with the aim of achieving equality of outcome is the main danger to the economic growth of the individual. The mere fact that some people in society own less property than others, they claim, is a good reason to try to equalize the difference between them.[126] A just government ought to treat everyone with equal consideration, and, they assert, doing so requires legislation aimed at the equalization of property.[127] This economic egalitarianism goes far beyond the uncontroversial claim that people should have equal political and legal rights.[128] Economic egalitarianism requires depriving the 86 percent of citizens who live above

---

[126] Kekes, John, "Dangerous Egalitarian Dreams", *City Journal*, Autumn 2001, https://www.city-journal.org/html/dangerous-egalitarian-dreams-12202.html. Article. Web.
[127] Kekes, Ibid.
[128] Kekes, Ibid.

the poverty level of a substantial portion of their legal owned property in order to give it to the 14 percent who live below it.[129] To deepen the analysis on economic egalitarianism, equality of outcome can only be applied through the exercise of a centralized government—a government that controls the means of production, like the one the Hamiltonian philosophy preaches. The control of the means of production is rooted in social welfare. Welfare is unfortunately, the element that entrenches the dependency of man to his government. I would even go far by saying that social welfare is the commencement of human enslavement in a free society. Even if egalitarianism could be defended philosophically because it has moral grounds, there is the small matter of implementing it in the real

---

[129] Kekes, Ibid.

world.[130] Just one reason the egalitarian dream cannot be realized involves what Robert Nozick called the "Wilt Chamberlain problem."[131] The Chamberlain problem could be explained this way; for instance, in Chamberlain's heyday, everyone enjoyed watching him play basketball.[132] People gladly paid to watch him play.[133] But suppose we begin with an equal distribution of wealth, and then everyone rushes out to watch Chamberlain play basketball. Many thousands of people willingly hand over a portion of their money to Chamberlain, who now becomes much wealthier than everyone else.[134] In other words, the pattern of wealth distribution is disturbed as soon as anyone engages

---

[130] Rockwell Jr., Llewllyn H. "The Menace of Egalitarianism", *Mises Institute,* October 8, 2015, https://mises.org/library/menace-egalitarianism. Article. Web.
[131] Rockwell, Jr., Ibid.
[132] Rockwell, Jr. Ibid.
[133] Rockwell, Jr., Ibid.
[134] Rockwell, Jr., Ibid.

in any exchange at all.[135] The reason the state holds up equality as a moral ideal is precisely that it is unattainable.[136] The government can portray itself as the indispensable agent of justice, while at the same time drawing ever more power and resources to itself—over education, employment, wealth redistribution, and practically any area of social life or the economy—in the course of pursuing unattainable egalitarian program.[137]

It is very important to remember that the goal of democratic socialism is to build a society based on egalitarian principles rather than that of libertarianism. A society that aims at achieving egalitarianism is bound to be subjugated to government tyranny, while the Constitution was precisely written in order to prevent tyranny from

---

[135] Rockwell, Jr. Ibid.
[136] Rockwell, Jr. Ibid.
[137] Rockwell, Jr. Ibid.

spreading within a free society. That is why I can personally asseverate with confidence that democratic socialism cannot and will never work in the United States of America.

References

Editors, "Alexander Hamilton", West's Encyclopedia of American Law (2005), The Gale GroupInc., https://www.encyclopedia.com/people/history/us-history-biographies/alexander-hamilton. Article. Web.

Editors, Ibid.

Editors, Ibid.

Editors, "Hamilton's Economic Policies", Dictionary of American History, (2003), The Gale Group Inc. https://www.encyclopedia.com/history/dictionaries-thesauruses-pictures-and-press-releases/hamiltons-economic-policies. Article. Web.

Editors, Ibid.

Editors, Ibid.

Editors, Ibid.

Editors, Ibid.

Editors, Ibid.

Editors, Ibid.

Editors, Ibid.

Franz, Joel, "Thomas Jefferson and Economic Policy" (2016), https://buzzazz.com/advertising-and-marketing/politics/jeffersonthomas-jefferson-and-economic-policy/. Article. Web.

Grampp, William, "Jefferson's Economics", Early Republican Economic Policy, Economic Liberalism, Vol.1 The Beginnings, Online Library of Liberty, (1965), https://oll.libertyfund.org/pages/early-republican-economic-policy. Article. Web.

Grampo, Ibid.

Grampo, Ibid.

Grampo, Ibid.

Grampo, Ibid.

Grampo, Ibid.

Grampo, Ibid.

Editors, "Allowing People To Decide or Decentralized Planning", Free Market Economics, December 2011, The Thomas Jefferson Center For ConstitutionalRestoration. https://thomasjeffersoncenter.com/2011/12/02/free-market-economics/. Article. Web.
Editors, Ibid.

Editors, Ibid.

Editors, Ibid.

Boaz, David, "Libertarianism", Encyclopedia Britannica, Politics. https://www.britannica.com/topic/libertarianism-politics. Article. Web.

Boaz, David, "Key Concepts of Libertarianism", Libertarianism: A Primer, Cato Institute, January 1, 1999, https://www.cato.org/publications/commentary/key-concepts-libertarianism. Article. Web.

Boaz, Ibid.

Boaz, Ibid.

Boaz, Ibid.

Boaz, Ibid.

Boaz, Ibid.

Boaz, Ibid.

Boaz, Ibid.

Boaz, Ibid.

Boaz, Ibid.

Boaz, Ibid.

Boaz, Ibid.

Boaz, Ibid.

Boaz, Ibid.

Friedman, Milton, "Understanding of Equality of Opportunity by Milton Friedman", Equality and Freedom, http://www.econ2u.com/friedman/understanding-of-equality-of-opportunity-by-milton-friedman. Lecture. Video.

Friedman, Ibid.

Editors, "Egalitarianism", Stanford Encyclopedia of Philosophy, First published in August 2002; substantive revision in April 2013. https://plato.stanford.edu/entries/egalitarianism/. Web.
Kekes, John, "Dangerous Egalitarian Dreams", City Journal, Autumn 2001, https://www.city-journal.org/html/dangerous-egalitarian-dreams-12202.html. Article. Web.

Kekes, Ibid.

Kekes, Ibid.

Kekes, Ibid.

Rockwell Jr. , Llewllyn H. "The Menace of Egalitarianism", Mises Institute, October 8, 2015,

https://mises.org/library/menace-egalitarianism.
Article. Web.

Rockwell, Jr. ,Ibid.

Rockwell, Jr. Ibid.

Rockwell, Jr., Ibid.

Rockwell, Jr., Ibid.

Rockwell, Jr. Ibid.

Rockwell, Jr. Ibid.

Rockwell, Jr. Ibid.

——————————

SIX

——————————

Bernie Sanders:
A Threat to Liberty
and
A Danger to Our Republic

Bernard Sanders, famously known as Bernie Sanders, who is the United States Senator from Vermont, has shaped the American political landscape through the 2016 election. Throughout the 2016 presidential election, Bernie Sanders became the sensational figure of the Democratic primaries. He is the political leader who has given a hard time to Hillary Clinton within the primaries. He did not run his campaign on the classical platform of the Democratic Party, which means with a moderate view on public policy. He radicalized his platform more to the Left and called it a political revolution. Bernie Sanders has been a United States Senator since 2007, but he came to national prominence during the 2016 election when he labeled himself as a "democratic socialist." Labeling himself as a democratic socialist, has gained him the support of the millennials. While delivering a lecture at the Institute of Politics at Georgetown University in November 2015, Senator Bernie Sanders explained what democratic socialism means. He stated:

"I don't believe government should own the means of production, but I do believe that the middle-class and the working families who produce the wealth of America deserve a fair deal."[138]

He expanded that statement by expressing what democratic socialism means to him. He declared:

"Democratic socialism means to me, building on what Franklin Delano Roosevelt said when he fought for guaranteed economic rights for all Americans. And it builds on what Martin Luther King Jr. said in 1968 'This

---

[138] Frizell, Sam, "Here's How Bernie Sanders Explained Democratic Socialism", Time, November 19, 2015, http://time.com/4121126/bernie-sanders-democratic-socialism/. Article. Web.

160

country has socialism for the rich and rugged individualism for the poor.' My views on democratic socialism builds on the success of many around the world, who have done a far better job than we have in protecting the needs of their working families, their elderly citizens, their children, their sick, and their poor. Democratic socialism means that we must reform a political system which is corrupted, that we must create an economy that works for all, not just for the very wealthy."[139]

The definition that Bernie Sanders gave, was everything but democratic socialism because democratic socialism is inherently incompatible with the democratic values of liberty, equality and solidarity. Bernie Sanders has repeatedly and relentlessly used Scandinavia as his empirical

---

[139] Lecture delivered by U.S. Senator Bernie Sanders at the Institute of Politics of Georgetown University, Washington, D.C. on November 19, 2015. https://www.youtube.com/watch?v=KQs_lmpQh6Q

evidence to support his definition of democratic socialism but as it was elaborated in the first chapter that, Scandinavian nation-states have a social democracy kind of regime instead of a democratic socialist system because Scandinavians do have a market-oriented economy with an amplified welfare state while democratic socialism rejects market economy. Before we even dig into Bernie Sanders political platform, there is one fundamental question that spurred my mind; why do millennials love Bernie Sanders? What do they see in him? Clearly Bernie Sanders was more popular than Hillary Clinton within the Democratic primaries in 2016. Following her defeat in the 2016 presidential election, Hillary Clinton has progressively faded off the public image and faded off the Democratic Party, which now makes Bernie Sanders the most likely Democratic politician to challenge Donald Trump in

2020 along with Former Vice President Joe Biden. When Bernie Sanders ran on the democratic socialist platform in 2016, he accentuated his campaign on three main issues; Income and Wealth Inequality, Free Education College Tuition and Debt Free, and Healthcare-For-All. These three issues have captivated the mind of the millennials. In 2020, he intended to run under that same platform. Now it is time to analyze these three substantial issues that would define a Sanders presidency and a democratic socialist system if it were to be one, according to Bernie Sanders.

Bernie Sanders believes that there is a significant problem of income inequality. The Vermont Senator claims that "In America, we now have more income and wealth inequality than any other major country on earth."[140] Bernie Sanders clearly exaggerates on inequality in America because he excluded nations such as Russia, Turkey and Brazil from his definition of "major."[141] According to the World Bank, at least forty-one counties in the United States have a better income inequality than Brazil, Chile, Argentina, or Israel.[142] And according to the most recent Global Wealth Databook, the United States ranks 16th out of 46 economies studies in the share of wealth held by the richest 1 %--Russia, Turkey, Egypt and Brazil are among those whose top 1 percent hold more than their nation's wealth.[143] So, Bernie's narrative on

---

[140] Jackson, Brooks, "Facts Check: Bernie Sanders Exaggerates Inequality", USA Today, May 29, 2015, https://www.usatoday.com/story/news/politics/elections/2015/05/29/fact-check-bernie-sanders-income-inequality/28086007/. Article. Web.
[141] Jackson, Ibid.
[142] Jackson, Ibid.
[143] Jackson, Ibid.

inequality of income is not objective but subjective and speculative. He [Bernie Sanders] exaggerated on income inequality strictly to win votes, and not because income inequality is or was at its all-time worst. According to Bernie Sanders, income inequality fosters an infinite spectrum of suffering.[144] While the middle-class gets smaller, the lower-class swells.[145] According to Sanders, failure to maintain a relatively equal distribution of income and wealth allows the rich to "buy elections," which allows them to exploit the political system, to rig the economy in their favor—and to prevent non-rich voters from doing anything about it.[146] To fix income

---

[144] Kolter, Philip, "Can we fix Income Inequality?", HuffPost, September 24, 2015, https://www.huffingtonpost.com/fixcapitalism/can-we-fix-income-inequal_b_8129972.html. Article. Web.

[145] Kolter, Ibid.

[146] Wilkinson, Will, "Bernie Sanders Is Right The Economy Is Rigged. He's Dead Wrong About Why", Vox, July, 15, 2016, https://www.vox.com/policy-and-

inequality, Senator Sanders believes that more regulations shall be implemented. That being said, he suggested the raise of the minimum wage, an increase in taxes on super-high incomes, a removal of tax loopholes, a penalty on companies for shipping overseas, provision of strong incentives for inner-city job creation, and the strengthening of laws on discrimination hiring, compensation, and promotion practices for women and minorities.[147] The fundamental producer of income inequality is freedom. Indeed, Individuals have different aptitudes and attitudes.[148] In an open society,

politics/2016/7/15/12200990/bernie-sanders-economy-rigged.
Article. Web.

[147] Kolter, Philip, "Can we fix Income Inequality?", HuffPost, September 24, 2015, https://www.huffingtonpost.com/fixcapitalism/can-we-fix-income-inequal_b_8129972.html. Article. Web.

[148] Will, George, "A Philosopher Takes On The Left's Obsession with Income Inequality", The National Review, October 18, 2015. https://www.nationalreview.com/2015/10/bernie-sanders-income-inequality/. Article.

rewards are set not by political power but by impersonal market forces, the rewards of which will differ dramatically but usually predictably.[149] Harry G. Frankfurt, professor emeritus of Philosophy at Princeton University, argues that inequality is not inherently morally objectionable.[150] Regulatory government inherently exacerbates inequality because it inevitably serves the strong—those sufficiently educated affluent, articulate, and confident to influence the administrative state's myriad redistributive actions.[151] When given a choice about how government should address the numerous economic difficulties facing today's consumer, Americans overwhelmingly—by 84% to 13%--prefer that government focus on improving overall economic conditions and the jobs situation in

---

[149] Will, Ibid.
[150] Will, Ibid.
[151] Will, Ibid.

the United States as opposed to taking steps to distribute wealth more evenly among Americans.[152] Americans' lack of support for redistributing wealth to fix the economy is reflected among income groups: upper-income Americans prefer that government focus on improving the economy and jobs by 88% to 10%, concurring with middle-income by 83% to 16% and lower-income by 78% to 17% Americans.[153] These findings clearly epitomized the stance of the American people on the redistribution of wealth. Although the majority of Americans agree that the government must provide incentive features to stimulate the economy; they, nonetheless, refuse that the government remains the main engine for the redistribution of wealth. It suggests that the

---

[152] Jacobe, Dennis, "Americans Oppose Income Redistribution To Fix Economy" Gallup, June 27, 2008, https://news.gallup.com/poll/108445/americans-oppose-income-redistribution-fix-economy.aspx. Article. Web.
[153] Jacobe, Ibid.

American people wants the market to endure the principal device of the means of production. Whereas Bernie Sanders claimed that he does not believe that government should own the means of production, if he were to become president, government would sooner or later, and therefore, inevitably become the owner of the means of production. As I have demonstrated in the previous essays, a government that owns the means of production is consequently a tyrannical government. A Sanders presidency would be a tyrannical presidency.

The second issue that needs to be analyzed, is the free-college tuition policy of Bernie Sanders. Senator Sanders has promised that if he were president, public higher education in America would be tuition-free, then more accessible to the poorest members of our society. The intent is surely good and characteristically genuine, nevertheless in public policy, intent does not prevail over effects. Notwithstanding the fact that emotion preponderates over reason in politics, emotion cannot subvert reason in public policy. In public policy, empirical evidences are the guardians of objectivity and truth. In public policy, we test sounded arguments and well-intended statements with empirical evidence in order to verify their validity. A sounding policy-proposal such as free-education does not necessarily mean that having a free-education system would deliver the great and positive results we expect. The analysis is to know how free higher education would substantially affect the economy—whether free college tuition would positively or negatively affect the national economy? The free-college tuition policy that Bernie Sanders wants to administer into our education system will substantively deteriorate the national economy. It will not advance the quality of education; it will neither create opportunity nor sustain equality. In fact, at only eighty schools—about 15 percent of four-year public colleges in the United States—did more than two-thirds of first-time full-time students manage to earn a degree within six years.[154] The graduation rates of the remaining 455 schools are so low that if they were high schools instead of colleges, they would be flagged as "dropout factories."[155] The plan of Bernie Sanders focuses more on the cost than the value of education, and that is deleterious. Empirical evidence and data from 2016 led by the U.S. Department of Education, demonstrates how the

---

[154] Camera, Lauren, "Free Tuition Isn't The Answer", US News, August 11, 2016, https://www.usnews.com/news/articles/2016-08-11/free-tuition-isnt-the-answer. Article. Web.
[155] Camera, Ibid.

price of education has little to do with the outcome. Indeed, at the average four-year public college, nearly 4 in 10 loan-holding students (36.5%) are unable to earn more than $25,000.00. six years after enrollment.[156] Higher cost for low—and moderate-income students does not deliver better results at our public institutions—the average net cost for those students remains virtually the same across the range of schools—whether students are graduating, finding employment, and paying back their loans or not.[157] The average top-quartile school charges a net price of $10, 176, while the average bottom-quartile school charges nearly $600.[158] The development of these findings expresses a serious decline in public

---

[156] Tamara Hiler, Lanae Erickson, "What Free Won't Fix: Too Many Public Colleges Are Dropout Factories", Third Way, August 11, 2016, https://www.thirdway.org/report/what-free-wont-fix-too-many-public-colleges-are-dropout-factories. Data.
[157] Tamara Hiler, Lanae Erickson, Ibid.
[158] Tamara Hiler, Lanae Erickson, Ibid.

education. Giving the increased focus on the rising costs of college and ballooning student debt, another important indicator of value is what percentage of an institution's student body is able to earn a decent salary and make payments on their post-enrollment.[159] Most students are choosing to go to college, first and foremost, to better their economic prospects by gaining expanded employment opportunities and access to higher wages.[160] Within the public educational system, not all public schools are equal. The cheaper price tag offered at most public colleges and universities often makes them a popular option for students and families looking to find a postsecondary education that will meet their educational and economic needs.[161] Public colleges and universities come in all shapes and sizes;

[159] Tamara Hiler, Lanae Erickson, Ibid.
[160] Tamara Hiler, Lanae Erickson, Ibid.
[161] Tamara Hiler, Lanae Erickson, Ibid.

undergraduate enrollment can vary from 200 to more than 50,000 students—most consumers have little understanding about just how wide—ranging their outcomes may be when they choose to enroll in a public university over another.[162] The inequality between public higher institutions also reflects a large gap in outcomes for students. This significant gap is underlined by the percentage of students earning more than $25,000 per year and the percentage of students able to enter into repayment on their loans.[163] By dividing the schools into quartiles, there is a 35.7-point difference between the average completion rate at top-quartile schools (66.5%) and the average completion rate at bottom-quartile schools (30.9%).[164] The disparity of outcomes within the public educational system in

---

[162] Tamara Hiler, Lanae Erickson, Ibid.
[163] Tamara Hiler, Lanae Erickson, Ibid.
[164] Tamara Hiler, Lanae Erickson, Ibid.

174

the United States indicates that the free cost of tuition does not guarantee an equal redistribution of outcomes for college-graduates. Furthermore, the findings of the Manhattan Institute for Policy Research showed that students in the lowest income brackets already receive enough federal and state grant aids to attend public institutions free of charge.[165] In Germany, for instance, where universities are tuition-free, only 28 percent of the general population has attained a college degree.[166] Researchers have found that free programs led to poorer attendance rates among secondary and postsecondary students.[167] If tuition is unregulated, low-cost or no-cost programs will likely experience

---

[165] Walsh, Jennifer, "Why States Should Abandon the 'Free College' Movement", The National Review, March 19, 2018, https://www.nationalreview.com/2018/03/why-states-should-abandon-the-free-college-movement/. Article. Web.
[166] Walsh, Ibid.
[167] Walsh, Ibid.

a type of "tragedy of commons" in which overconsumption leads to a depletion of resources and subsequent rationing of courses and programs.[168] When students are able to register with little or no personal cost, they may find it easier to walk away from a course or program than they would if they had to pay for it.[169] The plan of Bernie Sanders to implement free-tuition for higher education is quintessentially flawed and fallacious. The free-tuition college plan of Bernie Sanders will surely restrain one's liberty to choose. Sander's plan does not truly deliver tuition-free college for the exact same reason that the Affordable Care Act does not truly deliver universal health care: path dependency and reliance on state government

---

[168] Walsh, Ibid.
[169] Walsh, Ibid.

cooperation.[170] Sanders proposes using federal tax revenues to pay two-thirds of the current-in-state tuition if the state will contribute the other third from increased state appropriations.[171] Since states must contribute one-third of the revenue needed to make tuition disappear, this will require tax increase, or it will force states to move existing resources into higher education and away from other state priorities like healthcare, prisons, roads and K-12 education.[172] The Sanders proposal leaves out roughly half of the nation's colleges and

[170] Yglesias, Matthew, "there's a Big Problem With Bernie Sander's Free College Plan", Vox, March 14, 2016, https://www.vox.com/2016/3/14/11222482/bernie-sanders-free-college. Article. Web.

[171] David H. Feldman, Robert B. Archibald, "Why Bernie Sanders's Free College Plan Doesn't Make Sense", The Washington Post, April 22, 2016, https://www.washingtonpost.com/news/grade-point/wp/2016/04/22/why-bernie-sanderss-free-college-plan-doesnt-make-sense/?utm_term=.522f7da836b3. Article. Web.

[172] David H. Feldman, Robert B. Archibald, Ibid.

universities while adding a complex new set of federal rules for micromanaging the affairs of states and universities alike.[173]

The third issue that now needs to be addressed regarding Sanders' platform is "Medicare For All." "Medicare For All" is a single-payer healthcare system financed by taxes that covers the costs of essential healthcare premiums for all residents, with costs covered by a single public system.[174] Like socialism, which preaches the ultimate fulfillment of mankind in a utopian world, "Medicare For All" seems and sounds very good in the ears of the one who wish to remain delusive. George Mason University's Mercatus Center finds that Sanders plan would add $32.6 trillion to federal

---

[173] David H. Feldman, Robert B. Archibald, Ibid.
[174] "Single-payer system definition". September 23, 2017. Archived from the original on October 2, 2017. Retrieved December 12, 2017.

spending in its first ten years, with costs steadily rising from there.[175] The idea that a central government can plan 1/6th of the economy better than the private sector, for example, is belied by every other attempt at socialism.[176] Sanders wants to apply Medicare's below-market rates across the board, which would amount to a roughly 40 percent cut in payments to doctors and hospitals.[177] But cuts of that magnitude would drive doctors out of

---

[175] Editorials, "'Medicare For All' Would Cost $32.6 Trillion, And That's Not Even The Worst Of It", Investor's Business Daily, July 30, 2018, https://www.investors.com/politics/editorials/medicare-for-all-32-6-trillion-dollars-socialized-medicine/. Article. Web.
[176] Editorials, "Thank You, Bernie Sanders, For Exposing The True Cost of Socialized Medicine", Investor's Business Daily, https://www.investors.com/politics/editorials/thank-you-bernie-sanders-for-exposing-the-true-cost-of-socialized-medicine/. Article. Web.
[177] Editorials, "'Medicare For All' Would Cost $32.6 Trillion, And That's Not Even The Worst Of It", Investor's Business Daily, July 30, 2018, https://www.investors.com/politics/editorials/medicare-for-all-32-6-trillion-dollars-socialized-medicine/. Article. Web.

medicine and hospitals out of business, since the only way providers can afford Medicare's cut-rate reimbursements today is by charging private payers more.[178] The economic dynamics of a government-healthcare monopoly—like Britain's National Health Service—are tiresomely familiar: broad-based and heavy taxation and the imposition of government cost controls.[179] These controls may take the form of an overall spending limit or reductions in payments to health and medical providers.[180] If Sanders succeeds in imposing a federal monopoly on healthcare, no American would escape the damages.[181] His healthcare plan would replace the current system of private health insurers, which has

---

[178] Ibid.

[179] Moffit, Robert E. "Why Bernie Sander's Single-Payer Health Care Bill Would Be A Disaster", Fortune, August 21, 2017, http://fortune.com/2017/08/21/bernie-sanders-medicare-for-all-single-payer-health-care/. Article. Web.

[180] Moffit, Ibid.

[181] Moffit, Ibid.

seen healthcare costs continuing to rise.[182] As it may sounds attractive, the single-payer healthcare system that Senator Sanders wants to impose upon America is surely not the answer nor the right solution to ameliorate the healthcare system. If he were to be President of the United States under is democratic socialist regime, healthcare would be subsidized by the government, which would clearly affect prices. It implies that the government, as the largest purchaser of healthcare goods and services, can demand lower payments for services compared to private insurers.[183] But the lower payments of

---

[182] Anderson, Justin, "Medicare For All I Deeply Flawed: Media Forgets How math works", Salon, August 3, 2018, https://www.salon.com/2018/08/03/reporting-on-bernie-sanders-medicare-for-all-is-deeply-flawed-media-forgets-how-math-works/. Article. Web.

[183] Dana P. Goldman, Adam Leive, "Why 'Medicare-For-All' Is Not The Answer", Health Affairs, May 14, 2013, https://www.healthaffairs.org/do/10.1377/hblog20130514.031171/full/. Article. Web.

medical services would not reflect the quality of service because low payment of services equates bad performance due to limited resources. Moreover, the plan of Sanders would necessarily have an administrative cost under a democratic socialist regime. Medicare's low administrative costs—about 3 percent compared with 17 percent in the private sector—will have a detrimental effect.[184] The private sector relies on higher administrative costs to provide medical services because they use these funds to do a better job controlling excessive spending.[185] The healthcare plan proposed by Sanders has weaker incentives to limit high medical spending because everything will be at a lower cost, so which will incite the government to spend more. Meanwhile private insurers have become more

---

[184] Dana P. Goldman, Adam Leive, Ibid.
[185] Dana P. Goldman, Adam Leive, Ibid.

efficient, employing tools such as utilization review and case management to assess patient needs and then either restrict services or steer patients towards more cost-effective care.[186] The healthcare plan of Bernie Sanders overvalues lower costs over the quality of services, and that is a fallacious and dangerous factor that will inevitably harm the American people if his single-payer healthcare plan was invigorated.

The three issues upon which Bernie Sanders accentuates his agenda, spotlight a very invasive, intrusive, authoritarian and expansionary government. Like in a typical socialist system, the government of the democratic socialist regime of Bernie Sanders, will retain the means of production although he said that he does not believe that government should own the means of production.

---

[186] Dana P. Goldman, Adam Leive, Ibid.

You cannot promise a people to create a ton of government programs that would improve their lives without believing in controlling the means of production of these programs. It is nonsensical and illogic. Bernie Sanders is well aware that if he told the American public that he believes in the state controlling the means of production, his ideas would no longer have any value in the eyes of the general public. His solutions to tackle inequality of income, to provide free-higher-education-for-all, and affordable healthcare for all—will place government at the epicenter of all human activities in the United States. Economic activities will be controlled and subsidized by government. As I have numerously reiterated, the problem with government controlling the means of production is that—when the government, originally based on the principles of liberty, becomes the indispensable vector of economic power, it subsequently begins by imposing a coercive system that over time turns into tyranny. And the Constitution given to us by our Founding Fathers was strictly crafted to prevent tyranny from spreading over the republic. That is why Bernie Sanders is a clear threat to our liberty and a danger to our republic.

References

Frizell, Sam, "Here's How Bernie Sanders Explained Democratic Socialism", Time, November 19, 2015, http://time.com/4121126/bernie-sanders-democratic-socialism/. Article. Web.

Lecture delivered by U.S. Senator Bernie Sanders at the Institute of Politics of Georgetown University, Washington, D.C. on November 19, 2015. https://www.youtube.com/watch?v=KQs_lmpQh6Q

Jackson, Brooks, "Facts Check: Bernie Sanders Exaggerates Inequality", USA Today, May 29, 2015, https://www.usatoday.com/story/news/politics/elections/2015/05/29/fact-check-bernie-sanders-income-inequality/28086007/. Article. Web.

Jackson, Ibid.

Jackson, Ibid.

Jackson, Ibid.

Kolter, Philip, "Can we fix Income Inequality?", HuffPost, September 24, 2015, https://www.huffingtonpost.com/fixcapitalism/can-we-fix-income-inequal_b_8129972.html. Article. Web.

Kolter, Ibid.

Wilkinson, Will, "Bernie Sanders Is Right The Economy Is Rigged. He's Dead Wrong About Why", Vox, July, 15, 2016, https://www.vox.com/policy-and-politics/2016/7/15/12200990/bernie-sanders-economy-rigged. Article. Web.

Kolter, Philip, "Can we fix Income Inequality?", HuffPost, September 24, 2015, https://www.huffingtonpost.com/fixcapitalism/can-we-fix-income-inequal_b_8129972.html. Article. Web.

Will, George, "A Philosopher Takes On The Left's Obsession with Income Inequality", The National Review, October 18, 2015. https://www.nationalreview.com/2015/10/bernie-sanders-income-inequality/. Article.

Will, Ibid.

Will, Ibid.

Will, Ibid.

Jacobe, Dennis, "Americans Oppose Income Redistribution To Fix Economy" Gallup, June 27, 2008, https://news.gallup.com/poll/108445/americans-oppose-income-redistribution-fix-economy.aspx. Article. Web.

Jacobe, Ibid.

Camera, Lauren, "Free Tuition Isn't The Answer", US News, August 11, 2016, https://www.usnews.com/news/articles/2016-08-11/free-tuition-isnt-the-answer. Article. Web.

Camera, Ibid.

Tamara Hiler, Lanae Erickson, "What Free Won't Fix: Too Many Public Colleges Are Dropout Factories", Third Way, August 11, 2016, https://www.thirdway.org/report/what-free-wont-fix-too-many-public-colleges-are-dropout-factories. Data.

Tamara Hiler, Lanae Erickson, Ibid.

Tamara Hiler, Lanae Erickson, Ibid.

Tamara Hiler, Lanae Erickson, Ibid.

Tamara Hiler, Lanae Erickson, Ibid.

Tamara Hiler, Lanae Erickson, Ibid.

Tamara Hiler, Lanae Erickson, Ibid.

Tamara Hiler, Lanae Erickson, Ibid.

Tamara Hiler, Lanae Erickson, Ibid.

Walsh, Jennifer, "Why States Should Abandon the 'Free College' Movement", The National Review, March 19, 2018, https://www.nationalreview.com/2018/03/why-states-should-abandon-the-free-college-movement/. Article. Web.

Walsh, Ibid.

Walsh, Ibid.

Walsh, Ibid.

Walsh, Ibid.

Yglesias, Matthew, "there's a Big Problem With Bernie Sander's Free College Plan", Vox, March 14, 2016, https://www.vox.com/2016/3/14/11222482/bernie-sanders-free-college. Article. Web.

David H. Feldman, Robert B. Archibald, "Why Bernie Sanders's Free College Plan Doesn't Make Sense", The Washington Post, April 22, 2016, https://www.washingtonpost.com/news/grade-point/wp/2016/04/22/why-bernie-sanderss-free-college-plan-doesnt-make-sense/?utm_term=.522f7da836b3. Article. Web.

David H. Feldman, Robert B. Archibald, Ibid.

David H. Feldman, Robert B. Archibald, Ibid.

"Single-payer system definition". September 23, 2017. Archived from the original on October 2, 2017. Retrieved December 12, 2017.

Editorials, "'Medicare For All' Would Cost $32.6 Trillion, And That's Not Even The Worst Of It", Investor's Business Daily, July 30, 2018, https://www.investors.com/politics/editorials/medicare-for-all-32-6-trillion-dollars-socialized-medicine/. Article. Web.

Editorials, "Thank You, Bernie Sanders, For Exposing The True Cost of Socialized Medicine", Investor's Business Daily, https://www.investors.com/politics/editorials/thank-you-bernie-sanders-for-exposing-the-true-cost-of-socialized-medicine/. Article. Web.

Editorials, "'Medicare For All' Would Cost $32.6 Trillion, And That's Not Even The Worst Of It", Investor's Business Daily, July 30, 2018, https://www.investors.com/politics/editorials/medicare-for-all-32-6-trillion-dollars-socialized-medicine/. Article. Web.

Ibid.

Moffit, Robert E. "Why Bernie Sander's Single-Payer Health Care Bill Would Be A Disaster", Fortune, August 21, 2017, http://fortune.com/2017/08/21/bernie-sanders-medicare-for-all-single-payer-health-care/. Article. Web.

Moffit, Ibid.

Moffit, Ibid.

Anderson, Justin, "Medicare For All I Deeply Flawed: Media Forgets How math works", Salon, August 3, 2018, https://www.salon.com/2018/08/03/reporting-on-bernie-sanders-medicare-for-all-is-deeply-flawed-media-forgets-how-math-works/. Article. Web.

Dana P. Goldman, Adam Leive, "Why 'Medicare-For-All' Is Not The Answer", Health Affairs, May 14, 2013, https://www.healthaffairs.org/do/10.1377/hblog20130514.031171/full/. Article. Web.

Dana P. Goldman, Adam Leive, Ibid.

Dana P. Goldman, Adam Leive, Ibid.

Dana P. Goldman, Adam Leive, Ibid.

SEVEN

The Dictatorship of The Minorities:
The Subversion
Of Liberty
For an Egalitarian Society

One of the fundamental elements of American exceptionalism is the fact that the origin of the individual is not the main factor of his social elevation, nor that of his freedom. By origin, I mean the ethnic, racial, religious, and sexual background that constitute the package of one's identity. Compared to France, which has always had an assimilationist culture towards immigrants, immigrants in the United States do comply with the laws of the land while keeping their original culture. It does not make him any less American than the one born on American soil. The symbol of this American exceptionalism is rooted in cultural diversity because the United States is a pluralistically multi-racial and multi-ethnic nation. The greatness of American political culture is based on the fact that each individual is free to pursue his own interests so long as he does not encroach the freedom of others. It indicates that liberty and freedom are the main engines of the American collective advancement. The concept of cultural diversity is rooted in the precept of social inclusion. Indeed, the idea of cultural diversity in the United States has allowed the enlargement of social inclusion. If most immigrants seek to settle in the United States, it is because the principle of individual rights has always maintained the social order.

Over time, the American society has evolved in a regressive direction. The reason for this collective regression is grounded upon social inequalities. It is quite true that social inequalities are a real fact of the upheavals of our society. In its quest to reduce social inequalities, society has unfortunately embarked on the path to egalitarianism. Martin Luther King, Jr. did believe and fought for equality of opportunity because it is the most elemental right that humans living within a civil society could possibly have. He did not believe in equality of outcome nor in entitlements. Martin Luther King, Jr. believed that we, as a society, should not judge an individual by his physical appearance in order to give him treatment of favors at the expense of others, but we should judge an individual by the content of his character.[187] Judging an individual based on the content of his character promulgates equality of opportunity while judging one by his identity for the sake of giving him treatment of favor stimulates equality of outcome. A society that seeks egalitarianism aims to achieve two goals: equal redistribution of wealth, and equal

---

[187] Martin Luther King, Jr. "'I have A Dream' Speech", March On Washington (1963) https://www.archives.gov/files/press/exhibits/dream-speech.pdf. Discourse.

social justice. As I have already analyzed the economic aspect of the egalitarian society in the preceding essays, I will now dissect the social aspect of the egalitarian society under a democratic socialist system.

The precept of social justice in an egalitarian society is administered by a centralized government, which subsequently entails a very strong bureaucracy. The society in which we are currently living, is socially divided because we have abandoned libertarianism for the quest of egalitarianism. The quest for social justice to achieve equality has induced cultural separatism and thus the disintegration of the common good. Indeed, the individual of today's American society believes that the measurement of man's fulfillment is determined by his cultural identity. It means that, within an egalitarian society, cultural identity is the unit of measurement of man's worth. Nevertheless, we are all well aware that in a so-called free society like ours, the value of a human being is ascertained by the content of his character, which implies the assessment of his skills, abilities, and his capacity for objective judgement. Measuring man's value by his cultural identity subverts the potential and capacity that he has to offer on the market because there is no guarantee that because someone looks a certain way, that person will ultimately perform well. For example, being of Jewish origins does not automatically validate the superiority of intelligence of that person over a person of African origins. Jewish people are not naturally more intelligent than Blacks, nor that Blacks are not necessarily intrinsically more skillful than Jews. Each individual shall be assessed and judged objectively, based on the skill-set he has to offer rather than determining that person's worth based on speculative and unsubstantiated judgment.

Initially in the United States, the population was fundamentally composed of two distinguished social groups: a majority, mainly made of white individuals of European descents whether they were German, English, Irish, Italian, Polish, Swedish, or even Russian; and a minority comprised of all individuals from different ethnic background other that European descendance. Of course, the American society of the time was not perfect because two cultures; two civilizations had to learn how to live together within the same territory. And of course, there were flagrant and blatant inequalities in certain regions of the country, notably in the South with Jim Crow laws which relegated Blacks to second-class citizens. In order to have a more just society in which all members of society have the same rights to economic, social and political opportunities, Dr. Martin Luther King, Jr. fought for the Civil Rights Act to become law. It is essential to fathom that the philosophical goal of the Civil Rights Act of 1964 was to ensure that the value of the individual would be acknowledged by his talent, skills, and abilities. Notwithstanding that fact, the bureaucracy that followed the promulgation of the Civil Rights Act of 1964 has gradually distorted its [Civil Rights Act of 1964] philosophical purpose in order to strengthen the power of the federal government, and subsequently amplified its administrative control over the individual. The power of a centralized government is more effective when it is exercised over groups rather than individuals. In order to strengthen its administrative control over individuals, the centralized government has created minority social groups within the minorities. These minority social groups created and labeled as the "disadvantaged of society" are the Blacks, Asians, Hispanics, Native Americans, Indians (From India), Muslims, Jews, women, feminists, and LBGTs. By creating these social groups enunciated, the centralized government has inculcated in each of these groups— the narrative of social disadvantage. The rhetoric of social disadvantage is that if any of these groups is socially and economically lagging, it is not their own fault; it is because they are the victim of oppression from the majority (European white Christian male). Thus, the centralized government, by the primacy of social justice, is thereby presented as the defender of these oppressed groups. To appease their collective suffering and resentment, the government fabricates a system of social assistance in which the individuals of these social groups become increasingly dependent on it as if it were a drug. Of course, the main purpose of consolidating this social dependence has been to enable the government to carefully control the collective psyche of these social groups.

The distortion of the philosophical intent of the Civil Rights Act of 1964 enabled the centralized government to legitimize the victimization of minority groups. Minority groups have taken pride in their identity by substantively using the Civil Rights Act of 1964 as an asset to obtain preferential treatments. For example, Affirmative Action laws have prohibited universities from discriminating against a student of color or of different sexual orientation from minority group. These laws have consequently facilitated the admission of these students to prestigious universities, while some of them do not have the level required to cope with the educational standard of these institutions. This, clearly, epitomizes that some students from minority groups are admitted to a prestigious academic institution solely and strictly on the premise of their racial identity or of their sexual orientation. The worst is that if a university or an academic institution denies admission to a student issued from a minority group, that university or academic institution could be subjected to legal action and prosecution. For instance, a group of Asian Americans students have proceeded to legal action against the admission committee of Harvard University on the grounds that the university has denied their admission based on their skin color. But let me remind you here that Asians are the ones who have the best test-scores, they have the highest academic credentials within the national educational system. The case here is not about Asians being rejected because of their poor academic performances. It is quite the contrary. They have been denied admission because their outstanding academic performances prevent less-fortunate minority students to have access to quality education in prestigious academic institutions such as Harvard, Yale, or the University of Pennsylvania while these less-fortunate minority students may not necessarily be a good match for Ivy League schools since their academic standards might be lower than that of Ivy League's. Supporters of the lawsuit say Harvard illegally discriminates against Asian Americans, putting a cap on the number of Asians admitted to the university and making it harder for Asian applicants to get in.[188] Its opponents charged

---

[188] Wood, Josh, "The Wolf of Racial Bias: The Admissions Lawsuit Rocking Harvard", The Guardian, October 18, 2018, https://www.theguardian.com/education/2018/oct/18/harvard -affirmative-action-trial-asian-american-students. Article. Web.

that the case is not even about Asian Americans at Harvard; rather; they say it is an issue that has been co-opted by conservative activists whose real goal is to ending race-conscious admissions policies that give minority students a better shot at attending universities like Harvard.[189] Either way, race is the critical factor of this legal battle. Whatever the outcome of this case will be or could be, the focal point is here to illustrate how a university could be easily subjected to a lawsuit if it does not deliver the outcome instructed by Affirmative Action laws. These two examples on Affirmative Action substantiated how members of the minority groups optimized upon their cultural identity to obtain favorable or preferential treatments. The cultural identity factor as a result, has become perniciously the principal unit of measurement of man's value.

---

[189] Wood, Ibid.

Apart from the preferential-treatment policies introduced and invigorated by the government, the centralized government consolidates its administrative control over minority groups through a joint but restrictive narrative. This narrative is filtered through a set of keywords that the people can no longer use for fear of offending members of minority groups. However, this narrative informally known as political correctness, is a great danger to our freedom. Certainly, we, as individuals, are entitled and protected by the Freedom of Speech, which is a substantial feature of the First Amendment. Since political correctness has become the narrative of the mainstream culture, our rights to express our opinions has been severely undermined. As government controls the collective mind through the thread of political correctness, freedom of expression has been at risk. On the other hand, political correctness is also used by members of the minority as a weapon of retaliation. It signifies that any statement could be wrongly interpreted and can cause, sometimes lethal consequences, metaphorically speaking, such as employment's termination or being subjected to a lawsuit. This narrative, which was invigorated by the government in order to protect the "socially disadvantaged" and the "underrepresented," has in fact helped the government to consolidating its administrative control over social groups. Under such control, social minorities feel protected by the government against an oppression perpetrated by the majority (white male).

The quest for achieving an egalitarian society has detached the American people from their original premise, which is the preservation of liberty over tyranny. Today, the society wherein we are living is dictated and controlled by minority groups. These groups, through government, have now controlled the mainstream culture. The centralized government has made them believe that the value of man is determined by his cultural identity rather than the content of his character. It has indoctrinated these minority groups into believing that they are not able to succeed on their own expect through government support. This fallacious philosophy has indeed damaged the soul of American exceptionalism.

References

Martin Luther King, Jr. "'I have A Dream' Speech", *March On Washington* (1963) https://www.archives.gov/files/press/exhibits/dream-speech.pdf. Discourse.

Wood, Josh, "The Wolf of Racial Bias: The Admissions Lawsuit Rocking Harvard", *The Guardian*, October 18, 2018, https://www.theguardian.com/education/2018/oct/18/harvard-affirmative-action-trial-asian-american-students. Article. Web.

Wood, Ibid.

EIGHT

What Could Be Remembered?

Socialism has been; is probably; and will still be, the most powerful political ideology that has ever shaped the history of mankind. It is, as a matter of fact, the most powerful political doctrine in theory because its intention offers a paradise on earth that the human race could have never imagined. When Karl Marx and Friedrich Engels published *The Communist Manifesto*, they envisioned a new world order in which social classes and private property would be utterly eradicated. They envisaged a world in which the oppressed would become the rulers, by enslaving the aristocracy. Marx and Engels pictured a world in which the collectivization of the means of production would prevail over the free-market, so each member of society would obtain an equal redistribution of the wealth. In his book entitled *Capital: A Critique of Political Economy*, written in three volumes, Karl Marx used staggering and miraculous economic theories and formulas to demonstrate that capitalism and the free-market economy are the two fundamental foes of human fulfillment—that only a strong centralized economy based upon collectivism, could bring economic salvation and prosperity to the people. According to the proponents of socialism, a world order whereby every member of society is equal to one another, was worth trying.

Socialism in practice, has clearly been the antagonistic entity of its own theory. Indeed, the implementation of policies of collectivization have proven the opposite of its own theory. The majority of countries that have adopted socialism as their political and economic system, have resulted in two elemental failures: economic stagnation and dehumanization of society through political tyranny. As it was demonstrated in the previous chapters, nation-states such as the Soviet Union, Vietnam, Cuba, or Venezuela have resulted into economic stagnation because they all have a centrally-planned economy. The only beneficiaries of a society based upon a centralized economy are the government officials and the members of the bureaucracy who conduct the policies of the state. The masses who are supposed to be the first and main beneficiaries of the policies of the centrally-planned economy, are in reality alienated by the consequences of this economy. The redistribution of wealth is clearly inadequate and the economic disparity between the people and their sovereign is still much greater. The nationalization of the means of production inevitably leads to hyperinflation. This is today the case of the economic situation of Venezuela. Countries that have experienced socialism acknowledged that, in order to achieve equality, individual liberties and private property must either be restricted or completely abolished. In socialist regimes, individuals are serving the state instead of the state serving them. It entails that in a socialist regime, the state is substantively a coercive organ. It is more powerful than any other entity. If the state is more powerful than anything else, then none and no one can control the abuse of power perpetrated by the people running the state. The system of separation of powers is practically non-existent since all powers are concentrated and centralized in a single branch of government, which is the executive branch. The legislature and the judiciary in a socialist regime are subjected to the will power of the executive branch, because the executive power is the one that controls and enforces the policies to be implemented. The consolidation of administrative control over the means of production within the government inescapably suppress the political freedom of the masses. People have no right to protest, no right to retain ownership, no right to freely express their thinking, no right to freely vote, the press is censored, and journalists who write against the government's policies are systematically jailed and sometimes murdered. The concentration of government's powers in a socialist regime is so substantial that it is literally normal that it falls into tyranny. That is the reason why democratic socialism is a fallacy. It is probably the greatest fallacy in American politics because it attempts to portray a potentially-workable ideal in which democracy will prevent the socialist part of government to become a tyranny. It is impossible to be a democratic and socialist regime at the same time. Democracy preaches popular sovereignty and political liberty while socialism advocates for political equality and equal redistribution of wealth. Freedom and equality cannot both be maintained at the same level because one demands the restriction of the other. If we want more liberty and freedom (economic, political, and social liberty), then will certainly obtain inequality of production. If we want more equality, we will indisputably acquire a significant restriction of freedom. That being said, democratic socialism is therefore a political mockery, an illusion that seeks to indoctrinate the proponents of Keynesian economics, and an attempt to rehabilitate socialism, an ideology that has ultimately failed and will perpetually fail wherever it will be tried.

Democratic socialism can never work in the United States because the federal government is obligated to subject itself to the separation of powers doctrine, which is advocated by the Founding Fathers in the United States Constitution. As I said in the chapter entitled "The Roots of Libertarianism and Egalitarianism in America," the United States Constitution was written with a special and precise philosophical intent. This philosophical intent was, unequivocally, to deprive the federal government from substantive accumulation of powers so that it would not become a tyranny. Under the constitutional order, the three branches of government have well-distributed roles that allow none of the three branches to become more powerful from within than the other two branches. For example, if Bernie Sanders was president and wanted to administer socialized medicine, he would have to submit his bill to Congress. If he does not get the two-thirds of the votes in the House of Representatives and in the Senate, then his bill will not pass unless he signs an executive order, which will be an abuse of power. Adjunctively, the judiciary branch has the power and duty to verify the constitutionality of his [Bernie Sanders'] legislation. If the Supreme Court finds that his law is not in accordance with the constitutional principles of the republic, then the Court will declare his law unconstitutional. This example is to spotlight how difficult and nearly impossible it will be for democratic socialism to become an effective political and economic system in the United States. Bernie Sanders and his progressive henchmen are just sellers of illusions. They advocate platforms that are contrary to the principles of the American republic. The dissolution of the Soviet Union, the political and economic failures of Cuba, Venezuela, and Vietnam must serve as a lesson of history for all of us. Socialism, democratic socialism, and communism;

are political and economic doctrines that are doomed to fail no matter how many times we try to implement and regardless of the way we try to effectuate them. A doctrine that is designed to enslave man will always end up perishing itself because the ultimate purpose of man is happiness, and freedom is the highest form of happiness.

About the Author

Germinal G. Van is an author, essayist, and libertarian writer. He is a member of the Libertarian Party of Chicago, a member of the Midwest Political Science Association, and the policy advisor of libertarian political candidate Joshua Flynn, candidate for the Illinois State Legislature. He has published several articles for the *Libertarian Institute* and the *Foundation for Economic Education (FEE)*.

Mr. Van's works mainly focus on political philosophy, political economy, and social theory. He holds a bachelor's degree in political science from the Catholic University of America and a master's degree in political management from the George

Washington University. Mr. Van is the author of
several books.

Acknowledgements

The fulfillment of this manuscript would have not come to existence without the unconditional support of my wife Elise, and my sister Jennifer. I am tremendously grateful to them for their diligent assistance.

www.ingramcontent.com/pod-product-compliance
Lightning Source LLC
Chambersburg PA
CBHW070113260726
48658CB00001B/99